Grace, actually

Faith, Love, Loss
& Black Womanhood

Grace Sandra

Copyright © 2019 by Grace Sandra

All rights reserved. No part of this book may be used or reproduced by any means, graphic, electronic, or mechanical, including photocopying, recording, taping or by any information storage retrieval system without written permission of the author except in the case of brief quotations embodied in critical articles and reviews.

Cover Design by 100Covers.com
Interior Design by FormattedBooks.com

Author and Cover Photo by Grace Sandra

Dedicated to:
My three favorite humans.
Ransom, Rhys & Reverie.
Because of you, I've survived.

Table of Contents

Prologue vii
Misogynoir 1
    1 of 5 2
    2 of 5 9
    3 of 5 11
    4 of 5 16
    5 of 5 19
Faith 22
    1 of 2 23
    2 of 2 26
Loss 32
    1 of 4 33
    2 of 4 36
    3 of 4 41
    4 of 4 44
Love 49
    1 of 6 50
    2 of 6 51
    3 of 6 53

- 4 of 6 55
- 5 of 6 59
- 6 of 6 62
- **Heartache** **68**
  - 1 of 8 69
  - 2 of 8 77
  - 3 of 8 81
  - 4 of 8 88
  - 5 of 8 95
  - 6 of 8 98
  - 7 of 8 102
  - 8 of 8 105
- **Race** **115**
  - 1 of 5 116
  - 2 of 5 122
  - 3 of 5 124
  - 4 of 5 127
  - 5 of 5 129
- **Dem Babies** **132**
  - 1 of 4 133
  - 2 of 4 140
  - 3 of 4 145
  - 4 of 4 149
- **Acknowledgements** **155**

Prologue

This is my story and our story.

I started off as a "mommy blogger" on MySpace. Somehow, I managed to convince forty people to follow along. This felt super important, average as it was. So important I moved to Xanga, and after my first 100 readers, I made the move to Wordpress where I eventually held three different URLs. I never kept up with any of them, and they are now owned by businessmen in Taiwan whom I'd have to pay $600 to regain ownership.

That was back in 2008. I've basically been effing it up since then. By the by, I currently make my online home on Squarespace where tens of readers enjoy my choppy and inconsistent content on a blog I'm still unsure if I want to be about writing, activism, or lipstick. Like I said, it's complicated. Even though my online world is a mess, I can't not write.

My story is that I've rarely cared what the majority of people think of me at any given time. My ex-husband often accused me of "personality crafting" online—try-

Prologue

ing like hell to shape an opinion of myself I approve of—when, truthfully, I've told my story with little regard for what folks make of it. (Repeat: *little* regard versus *no* regard.) It's been several years since those comments were made; he's still wrong. It mattered little to me that he and others misunderstood my intentions to share vulnerably, shown largely by the fact that I continue to do it. Honestly, I destest when folks use their uncomfortability of my vulnerability to attempt to silence me, their reasons as absurd as the day is long.

My story is that I have *little* interest in hiding. I could go all Brene' Brown on you, but it's bigger than merely wanting to live wholeheartedly. Hiding is exhausting, especially when you enjoy sharing your life with others. Don't assume that people who have no interest in hiding are a much broker version of Kim Kardashian. Obviously, women like Kim and I share a certain level of defiance to continue to put all our business on all our platforms.

Let me be clear, unless otherwise stated, it is ridiculous for anyone to tell myself, Kim Kardashian or anyone in between *what* our motives are, *why* we should (or shouldn't) disclose in the way we do, and exactly what *they think* about our levels of disclosure. Unless it's explicitly stated, never assume you know why anyone shares a great deal of their life online. Some of us enjoy it, even as we fuck up our lives and our platforms while we're at it.

My story is that I learned a great deal from Malcolm X. I read his book as a young pimple-faced teen. He was a man who put out all his business and shared it on his literal platform because he believed in the power of storytelling. He wanted folks to know the exact reasons he continued to fight for justice for his people. He didn't let anyone tell him to shut it down because he took ownership of his choices. He didn't want to leave room for someone to catch him off guard, therefore, gaining power over him. No one had anything on him that he hadn't already shared. If I'd been around when Malcolm X was alive, I definitely would have slid in his DMs with an inappropriate shot of my non-existent ass for which he would have appropriately blocked me. #LittleBootiesMatter

My story is that I'm an adult survivor of severe childhood sexual abuse. That I'm "surviving" feels precariously up for grabs.

My story is that I share my vulnerable stories over and over, and women connect with me to thank me. At first I felt pressure, but now I understand sharing is the gift that keeps on giving. When I was sixteen, I made an important decision: dark secrets in the dark don't get to live in me. It is unfair to myself and others who genuinely need to hear the truth.

My story is my horribly-dysfunctional relationship to my sexuality. Hi. I'm Grace, and I'm a sex addict. More specifically, I'm a love addict, which falls under the umbrella of sex addiction. I'm not addicted to sex, per se. I don't sleep around. I've never been to a strip club nor shoved a dollar down anyone's dirty draws. I've never paid anyone to sleep with me, though I have begged my ex a time or two. I'm not addicted to porn or masturbation or any other thing you imagine when you think of sex addiction. I'd never even heard of the phrase until David Duchovny came out as one. I assumed the worst of him for forty-eight hours, then forgot. But I'm the real deal. Just like David, I sent myself away to a fancy camp for "women like me." I attended a camp I refer to affec-

Prologue

tionately as "Sex Camp." (There is no sex at sex camp, you cheeky bastards).

How does a 39-year-old wife, minister, and mother get diagnosed with sex addiction? It's a story best told at the beginning. It started many years ago with my first sexual partner—my Dad. He began sexually assaulting me when I was three years old and continued for eight years. Let's just assume that fucked me up. I didn't understand *exactly* how it fucked me up until I'd pretty much fucked up my entire life. That's a lot of fucking. Ba-doom-ching! Sorry, that's a sex addict joke. I kid.

For years I white-knuckled this love/sex addiction thing. Issues with my sexuality were always bigger than me. The only way I knew something was wrong was how seemingly simple interactions, sex or relationsihps with men had the power to upend my whole life. I gave my power and my body away as if I was handing out free t-shirts.

Then, I experienced a reprieve: a few years of awesome, married sex followed by a few years of a confusing relationship with a man (not my husband) which led to a few months of us having an affair, followed by a few months of profound guilt and shame. Then, I was date raped. Finally, I experienced a few more punishing years of sexual abandonment and rejection by my second soon-to-be-ex-and-currently-separated husband. It's been a real shit-show—one that's mostly focused on my vulnerabilities and my penchant for allowing abuse. I never got ahead of it. Until now. At 42, y'all. 42. My freedom is several decades in the making.

Year after year I made small, seemingly-inconsequential choices to face my demons again and again. I decided to do whatever it takes for over twenty years. It's takes

Grace Sandra

an amazing woman to make choices that both served me, right alongside choices that destroyed me, and have them somehow balance out in such a way that I've neither killed myself nor experienced much success. As a result I became amazingly mediocre; my disjointed relationships with men an ever present reminder that I continuously allow myself to be destroyed by own greatest weakness.

There are those of us who don't believe we're deserving of a good life, so we sabotage the bejeezus out of it. Sometimes, people know they aren't deserving of a horrid life and claw like hell to survive it all. Sometimes, people do both. I could never decide if I was worthy of a man who truly loved me or even to keep $100 in my savings account. But once I thought I might lose my children, all of a sudden *I knew* I was deserving of better. I never failed to acknowledge my flaws, while simultaneously knowing I wanted more. One thing about me. I have found myself in dysfunction time and time again but I decided never to stay there.

My story is that my issues have very little to do with you, my friends—past and present, nor my past partners or husbands. Friends centered themselves in my story because my choices affected them. It's understandable, but wrong. Also, codependent. You may have life-long issues that have very little bearing on your current-day relationships, and yet, folks will insert themselves as if you have inherited the role of godmother and must nurse them back to health. Here's what seems to work. Ask them to stop, please. Ask them to figure out how to love you through your issues, brokenness, and pain, or let you off the hook. If they will not agree, walk away first.

My story is that I am unwilling to allow "friends" to center themselves into it. My story is that having an affair, two fucked-up marriages, and a broken-ass sexuality creates an insane amount of consequences all by itself. I'm not willing to tolerate folks centering themselves in my story and hurting me more as a result. I have lost friends on this journey because of centering. Most of them white women. Stated as pure, ironical observation.

My story is that I allow people to challenge me when said in love and with a modicum of understanding and compassion. I can give you 10 real names of real people who have helpfully challenged me, thus catapulting my growth.

If people throw centering garbage my way? I am done. That is the end of our story. I have survived too much damn trauma to tolerate those who cannot communicate without heaping shame and pain. I'd rather face the loss of a friendship than allow a friend to re-traumatize me.

My story is that I am God's daughter; perhaps God has allowed me to stoop so low so I could begin to understand the amazing grace with which I've been operating all these years when I was everyone's Favorite This! and Up and Coming That! It's hard to see your need for a Savior when you're at the top of the heap. Here I am at the bottom, and my story is that I'm more in awe of God than ever before. God saved a ratchet ass like me.

My story is important. If it makes you feel uncomfortable, dig deep, friends. Find out why. When I own my words and choices and find the bravery to share them, it frees me. When I write them, I learn from them; when I share them, I offer them.

Your story is important. Tell it. Write it. Learn from it. Share it. Offer it. Find the bravery to free yourself, to own your choices, and to create agency for yourself. Don't let folks center on you.

Grace Sandra

Those of us in the world who call ourselves "storytellers" join in on the attributes of God himself, the greatest storyteller of all time. And that is grace. Amazing Grace.

Life is our story to tell. Come join me in a bit of mine.

This book is a compilation of my most popular blog posts and articles and several journal-y pieces I wrote for myself and never published anywhere.

Enjoy. Or don't. Up to you. It's all grace, actually.

I'm a Beyonce fan. There seems to be levels to my fandom. For much of her career, I was a low-to-mid-level fan. I've never been to a concert, but I do purchase her albums. I stalk her on Instagram, but I've never spent time defending against trolls. I love althleisure, but own no Ivy Park. *Lemonade* changed all that for me. Now, I'm dying to get to a concert, and I'll argue or debate anybody seeking to dismiss the raw beauty and vulnerability she shows and how she's incorporating activism into her visual artistry and lyrics.

I expected to watch *Lemonade* for the first time as merely a pleasant and enjoyable viewing. I didn't know what I was about to experience.

I'd read that *Lemonade's* concept was being described as "every woman's journey of self-knowledge and healing." That statement is the whole truth and nothing but. The journey those tracks took me on was one I related to in more ways than I expected.

I am an ethnically Black and Italian light-skinned woman who racially identifies as a Black-American. *Lemonade* reminded me of the questions constantly swirling through my head: *how am I a black woman? How am I biracial woman? What's the difference? The predominant questions being: I'm biracial, but ain't I black woman, too? Does the whole of me fit into the black experience of women across America or nah?*

Watching *Lemonade,* I found myself in it. It's okay that I don't easily align exactly with the blackness I see in others. I contemplated how split in two I've felt. When I was with my first husband who is white, I felt black... blacker, I suppose. When I was with my second husband who is black, I've felt white...whiter, I suppose. When I realized racial identity was all tangled up in how others viewed me next to them, it felt heavy. At the same time, my entire life, I've never not felt black, nor have I benefited from any of the same privileges that white women do. Though I know I benefit from light-skinned privilege.

My black soon-to-be ex-husband never communicated his surprise over some new element of my personality or viewed my preferences as a mark off my black card. He joked about *my inner white girl* which I took umbrage in because I understood what he saw.

I was raised by a white woman, exclusively. My black father spent eleven years of my childhood in prison. I had no access to him, my black family members, nor his cultural tutelage beyond ten years old. My mother sent me to an all-white, private Christian school seeped in a conservative Baptist tradition, and we attended their accompanying large Baptist Church. We spent Wednesday nights at Awana, a program for youth designated to memorizing Bible verses and running around primary-colored circles. When they say it takes a village to raise a child, it's true. My mother made sure my primary village was 100-percent white without exception.

If I think too long and hard about it, I have a *Fight Club* confusion about it all.

That white village didn't protect me from the experience of being a young, black woman in America. In fact, that white village did everything it could to ensure I knew just how exclusive it was. That white village made for damn sure I knew I was among them, but not one of them. When I was told I was not allowed to be baptized in that white church on account of being black, my heart experienced the first tightening of the lynching cord. And when in the seventh grade my best friend told me I couldn't come to her birthday party because her mom didn't allow blacks in her home, the noose burned a bit tighter. Her father sat on the school board and was a prominent leader in the church. By the time I was 11, I understood the implications that structural, systemic racism runs deep.

As the years went by, the village became more suffocating, and the noose tightened. When my older brother from my mother's first marriage—a white man—often referred to me as a nigger in our home, I got a quick lesson of what an oppressive, emotional lashing felt like.

He often accompanied his rabid use of the word "nigger" with "stupid," and even though I can only remember him referring to me as a "stupid little nigger" a handful of times, I will never forget the numerous times and ways I heard him use it in our home. After every news story, "Those niggers...look what they did." After anything happened to our house or cars, "It was the niggers' fault." He was relentless. He warned me against becoming a stupid-ass nigger, talking and walking like a nigger.

In fact, he was the only white person in my life who held out hope that I'd see myself exclusively as white, denying my blackness altogether. As messed up as it is, he was the sole white person to ever communicate, albeit in a sick and twisted way, "Grace, you are welcome to be white like me." In essence, he asked of me, *Please, be white.*

I have lived my entire life being sure to respond to him and anyone else requiring that passive-aggressive demand: "No, thank you."

No, thank you. I do not want any part of whiteness of which you remain inexplicably proud.

In school, the girls never hesitated to point out differences: "Why is you hair so...greasy?" they'd lament with disgust. I knew several girls whose fathers told them if they brought home a black boyfriend, he would be met with a shotgun at the door. Thus began the fear that most black women feel at every point in their life: that every black man they know and love is susceptible to the antics, fears, suspicions, violence, and hatred of reckless, white men, which history has yet to disprove. I felt the angst of little, white boys who I wanted to like me but found me gross: my hair, my skin, my poverty. I lived IN Detroit. The *actual* city of Detroit. I was shipped to this school like an Amazon box while they were suburban kids with a fear of Detroit like I fear a snake pit. I was raised in this village, but I was not safe in this village. This village gave me a huge lesson in whiteness that caused me to repulse it and despise the parts of me which mimicked it.

Meanwhile, in my urban center, my circle of black friends in my black neighborhood contributed to a growing sense of my inclusion to the whole of blackness in America. I can't remember the number of times I was strongly corrected by an older child or adult when someone would ask me "what I was" and I'd say "mixed." They'd cut me off with a fierce passion, "No! You black!" The one-drop rule was heavily in place in my Detroit neighborhood.

If you have one drop of black blood, you are blackety-black, which was fine by me. I wanted nothing more than to distance myself from all white people everywhere, all of them with one problem or another with the minuscule amount of blackness they saw in me and the pervading blackness they saw in Detroit, which they obviously feared. I pitied and loathed them and hated many of them even while embracing a few dear ones.

The neighborhood kids sat around talking about racial issues. With our limited perspectives and young minds, all we knew was the racism we'd experienced. I'm not sure we even used that word, but our experiences could be summed up this way: shit hurt. I didn't know how to articulate how sad and sorry my weak-ass, white village was. I only knew that every day I was a part of it, I hurt. Somehow, instinctively, in my gut, I felt the brunt of their racist bullshit even when it was the most covert undercover b.s. the North has ever seen. I felt it uniquely among my black peers on the block. All of them went to 98-percent-dominantly black schools where they were saved from interacting with racist, white Christians, the worst kind of racist white folks in my opinion. I'll take a racist atheist any day.

Grace Sandra

Where was my inner white girl then? What did my inner white girl do to save me from all that noise? What did having a white mother or light skin do to keep me from the pain of my primary village teaching me directly about racism? Does my light skin prohibit me from experiencing the fullness of the black experience? Has it protected me so far? No. I will acknowledge the inherent privilege of this skin. All day, every day, I will speak of how it benefits me over my darker-hues sisters. I will carry the extra burden and shame of walking every day with this skin in a system that privileges me that I did not create but hope to dismantle.

As I watched *Lemonade,* all at once, I felt I had lived the fullness of the black woman's experience. Despite my inner white girl, my light skin, my white mother, my enjoyment of Britney Spears' albums, I had lived and felt the similar sting of Beyonce's journey.

Ain't I a black woman?

Haven't I felt the lash?

Haven't I been denied the humanity?

Haven't I watched a black man being ripped from my arms into the system?

Don't I love a black man who lives under the weight of being feared?

Don't I know the sting of betrayal?

Haven't I longed for the safety of the sisterhood?

Haven't I looked at white women with both awe, despair, jealousy, pity, envy, anger and adoration?

Is not my confusion a valid experience?

Haven't I been forced to make lemonade out of America's lemons?

Ain't I a black woman, too?

Yes, yes I am.

I am God's daughter. Detroit's daughter. A black daughter. A beloved daughter. A prodigal daughter. A daughter of a father and a mother. I have liberty, the spirit of adoption and acceptance! I love God with my whole heart.

I am an advocate. A wounded healer. I bring grace, empathy, and compassion.

I am a communicator of God's love for the poor, but especially the poor in spirit.

I am a lover of His Word.

I am Esther for such a time as this. I influence. I inspire. I am God's mouthpiece, who He uses.

I am a strong and brave bearer of the mantle of reconciliation. My blood and DNA is a testament to the power of reconciliation among black and white Christians.

I am a sister in Christ, a mother in Christ, a lover in Christ.

I am a recipient of his restoration: heart restoration, identity restoration.

I am a Prophetess. A prophetic teacher. I am called for a purpose to bring His good news to a lost generation.

I am she who forgives the men who have sexualized me, who have brutalized me, who have beaten me.

I have not been consumed when the fires have blazed all around me. I have not been abandoned by God in the pit.

He has allowed me to be burned but not consumed. I bear scars and have been broken but kinsikori—I am more beautiful for having been broken.

I am authentic. I radiate.

I am a hope pointer. A harbinger of God's grace.

I am braver than I believe, stronger than I seem, and smarter than I think.

I am to leave a legacy for my children.

I am not left without hope.

At all times, I walk in abundance.

I needed a change. Usually, when I need a change I big chop. I've big chopped five or six times in the last few decades.

My first big chop came after I got dumped by the first guy I thought I'd marry. Several years later, I big chopped a few days after my first miscarriage in a pregnancy I desperately wanted. The next time was after my Dad died. His death was significant only in the fact that I suddenly felt like the world was a safer place.

In hindsight, I'm not certain if my big chops helped me cope better or not. If anything, it amplified the pain of loss. I had hair, then I didn't. All of a sudden there was nothing to hide behind. I'm not sure why we mourn this way, ladies. Though I understand it to be effective for some, I've realized it's not a good coping tool for me.

I've decided to never again make big hair transitions after facing life's hardships.

My junior year in college I tried something new, a cute little Halle Berry, pin-straight pixie cut. Bruce, my stylist, suggested I go for platinum highlights. I didn't think much of it and gave him the go ahead. After it was done, I looked, well, white. For the first time in my entire life, I was passing for a full-blooded, 19-year-old white woman. It was nuts. People were treating me differently—*better,* I should clarify. Black people were calling me white, something I'd never heard in my life. Even though I'm a high yellow, redbone, I'd never passed. Not ever. A full-on, existential identity crisis ensued. Within one week, I went back to Bruce and made him turn my hair back to black.

After my first divorce, I was tempted to reach for the scissors. My hair was as long as it had ever been. I'd been natural for years and had finally learned to manage it. I decided to switch up my normal black and make a large chunk of the top blond. While I was there, I decided to get a blowout, too. Two weeks of blowout bliss seemed good for the soul. Because of what happened in college, the plan was to go immediately back to my natural curls.

At the time, I was a moderately well-known blogger with an active social media presence. I wasn't sure anyone cared about my hair. I wrote a blog post preemptively, to cut off any suspicions of why my black, natural hair was suddenly blond and straight. I thought it would be enough to explain I needed a brief change and didn't want to big chop. It was not enough. The internet lit up my ass. I was accused of wanting to look white, wanting to be white, betraying my blackness, betraying others' blackness, hating my natural hair, hating myself, and being an idiot. One black man told me I was a sad excuse of a black woman, which is, frankly, obnoxious.

In my writing career, I've taken on heavy topics. I'm accustomed to some negative feedback. I don't have thick skin, per se; my little feelings still get hurt, but I've understood pushback is a part of the game. This felt different. The commentary became so personal on something so impersonal to them. They didn't have to wear my new do. How could they possibly know my motives without asking?

After the fallout, I thought about famous mixed race people who present in a variety of ways: Halle Berry, Barack Obama, Mariah Carey, Zendaya, Bob Marley, Boris Kodjoe, Stacey Dash, Tracey Ellis Ross, Derek Jeter. Like me, they all have one white parent and one black parent. Would it be okay for any of them to be perceived as white? Folks seem comfortable calling President Obama black, but I've rarely heard of Derek Jeter being referred to that way. Same thing with Mariah Carey. Us super-light-skinned folks get all caught up in the middle, and in some cases, judged far more harshly. *How dare you be able to pass, you uppity-ass, passin'-ass negro!*

The feedback was tough, but the truth was I didn't like it either. I took way too many selfies trying to find myself in this altered state. If I looked hard enough, I might see the woman I wanted to be peering past straight, blond hairs. I did feel white(r). I did feel *too different*. Too much. Too blond. Too vulnerable even for Instagram. By the by, I went back to curly within a few weeks and back to black within a few months.

It did not matter why I straightened my hair or dyed the top portion of my head blond. It did not matter if I looked white or was perceived as white. It did not matter if I wanted to look white or actively avoiding looking white. It does not or should not matter to me what anyone else in the world thinks about something as superfluous as my hairstyles, which are prone to change often.

The style didn't mean I was ready to Beyoncify myself. I was not trying to make a grand statement. It's just hair. I wanted a change. That is all. Since then, I've tried pink, purple, teal, and green. Hair color is mostly a reflection of my mood and confidence. Because I'm an enneagram 7, I fear boredom like the plague. I have to change my hair regularly, or I will die of boredom; it's a scientific fact.

I am not my hair, though I feel the tug of war as a black-identifying woman where the weight of others perceptions of me, my body, my personhood, and my hair are parsed out, usually publicly on a scale to determine my worthiness.

The judgment starts with hair. Take Beyonce's daughter Blue Ivy, for example. As soon as we grow ass and titties, the judgment morphs into an all-encompassing movie reel of contempt. Any choice I make regarding my sexuality, hair, shoes, or clothes feels weighted. My perceived value is dependent on whether or not I am labeled strong and beautiful by black men, nice and pleasant by white women, and successful or intelligent by white men.

Black women damn ourselves if we step out of those those carefully-manicured roles. When we do, they call us hood-rats or video vixens. On the opposite side, we're called angry black women or an uppity, black bitches. You can't win. I can't win. We all know that. I will never win in the court of public perception, no matter what my hair is doing. There is no point in trying.

Grace Sandra

As a biracial woman who identifies and is primarily identified as a black woman, I've been working on truly loving myself for the way I look for several years. My beautiful yellow, super-light-skinned self lacks a significant portion of melanin I wouldn't mind having a bit more of, especially during long Michigan, sunless winters.

Yet, this is how God made me. I recognize I benefit from light-skinned privilege. It is absolutely real. I have to dismantle the lies within myself and the lies I others assign to me based solely on the shade of my skin color. I abhor colorism within the Black American community, and it needs to end. I understand how we got here, I understand why we are still here, but I hope we can put it to bed eventually. I hope we can see it for what it is: another iteration of boring-ass, tired-ass lies whispered in our ears for 400 years to divide and subjec

I wrote this for Dajerria Becton shortly after a viral video in June 2015 showed a white police officer in McKinney, Texas, raise his baton towards her, drag her by her hair, slam her into the ground, pin her tiny, vulnerable, 15-year-old body to the ground while she shrieked out, "I want my Mama."

-

Your necessary air is restricted. You take short breaths. You wait for relief. One day, it hurt so bad you took a viability assessment. Will you live?

Verdict's out.

There's a goddamn boot on your neck. *One day, it will come off,* you reason. You wait. One day, you'll take a long, deep breath. Until then, short, quick breaths are gold. Just survive.

Grace Sandra

It's been so long, this boot made its home. You've re-adjusted. You will live, boot-in-neck. You will live. Boot-in-neck living is your new normal; rather, your *only* normal. You take the quick, fear-laced breaths because *you have to.*

You grab the boot. You dig in your fingernails, you dig elbows into the ground. Aided by leverage, you push. You push hard. There's one glorious second. A single moment exists, frozen in time, and you breathe.

You BREATHE!

The air flows in with a gush, your lungs expand, the relief mighty. The boot responds accordingly. It turns right, then left, grinding down harder in angry fear: SHUT THE HELL UP!

You are not silenced. You've breathed out life made possible by grit and raw courage.

The boot pushes. Your throat constricts uncomfortably, dreadfully, into your esophagus. You have less air now than before, but what was your option?

Would you lay still, wasting limited breath on defeated tears? No. You push the boot for good reason.

You need one moment in time to breathe deeply. You grasp hold of humanity and reason. You dig in manicured nails. Your seemingly insignificant act of boot pushing communicates, *I AM HERE, dammit!* Your strength in leverage articulates: *WORTH! STRENGTH! There is dignity in my hands!* You push up on the boot because longer breath gives way to healing tears, and even those don't come for free.

Not for you.

You glance to your right and to your left. You see rows upon rows of others lying under the boot. In sporadic bursts, elbows dig, grunts, and sweat deliver pushes and heaves for a moment's worth of sweet relief all around you. Boots grind, anger stomps the life out of some, but for those among you who survive, you keep pushing, grunting, digging, fighting, dying. Just as you've always done, strong black woman.

Just as you've always done.

You've mastered suffocation *while* you live. The boot isn't merely your new normal. The *only thing new* was The Moment of Realization: *I have a boot on my neck?!*

You acknowledge reality. You meet eye-to-eye with the one next to you, you clasp dirty fingernails and sweaty hands, and you push.

Just as you've always done.

Just as you always will.

#SayHerName

When there's an enormously unbalanced out-of-wedlock birth rate among African-American women, why doesn't the problem also lie with the men who fuck us?

The men who insert their penises, knowing good and doggone well the action could bring life?

But it's also the men who rape us.
It's the men who take advantage of our obvious vulnerabilities.

It's our fathers.
Our brothers,
Our uncles, and
our cousins.

Did we not grow up with these men touching us anywhere and everywhere?

And if they didn't touch us, didn't they tell us in so many words,
What can that ass can do?

And didn't we watch them watch older women?
And didn't we hear them cat call?

And didn't we see them cheat with the white women and feel the pang at our 10-year-old, nappy fro, already not good enough?

And did we ever hear them say who we were outside of our sexuality?

And was there any other action to help us figure out what we had to offer?

I mourn for us black women because we are almost always the *only* ones who say:

Black girls are magic.
Black girls rock.
Black women have incredible strength and resiliency.
Our lives matter.
Say her name.
Black women are incredible gifts to humanity.

There are some black men who say this. A limited number. But the rest? They say in word and deed:

Grace Sandra

You are not *actually* wanted.
You are not chosen.
You are not worthy of protection.
You are not the type of beauty I desire.
You are a hoe.
You are a thot.
You are a bitch.

I remember meeting Jesus once at sex camp. It wasn't our first meeting, but an important one.

Everyday I walked up to a giant, beautiful, colorful painting of Jesus' head, hair blowing in the wind. The massive painting hung on the wall of the church where I was attending a week-long retreat for women being treated for female sex addiction…what I like to call "Sex Camp."

When I first saw the painting I was taken aback. Great art captures one that way. And the size, my God, it was huge. "Well, hello there Jesus," I said. In that moment he seemed so real with his piercing brown eyes bigger than my head.

In the course of the week, every time I passed it I'd say, "Hey, Jesus! Another great day at sex camp!" I'd try to say sweetly but somewhat sarcastically. "How are you feeling about sex camp?" "Me?" "Oh, well I feel deep shame and loathing self-pity, so there's that. I'd rather be on a cruise. No offense."

I could not help but smile at this morning ritual. There was Jesus. His face so colorful, the painting as large as the wall felt much like his presence in my life: always in my face, pretty but comfortably hovering. I stopped to look at the painting and began to sit with it several times throughout the week. His head was made of every paint color the artist could think of, which did not show him as a blond with blue eyes, pleasing me to no end.

There was Jesus at sex camp, with this ominous happy smirk as if he was singing the tune of Mr. Rogers' Neighborhood. He was welcoming. It did not surprise nor shame me that Jesus was here at sex camp. *Where in the fuck else should Jesus be than at sex camp* with a bunch of adulteress, whoring, cheating, slutty women who the world views as hoes, thots, tramps, hood-rats, and sluts that have been ran through so many times we are found to be of the most heinous variety of women alive? The only Jesus I've every known is exactly the one who would show up at a week-long rehab for female sex addicts. And He showed up in more ways than in a wall-size painting. I have more stories of meeting Jesus at sex camp than I have time to write.

The painting stood as a beacon of hope for me that week, tethering me to the reality of His presence amidst the exposure of my deepest shame. If the painting had not been there, what other symbols would I have grabbed onto? Every break, every morning, every meal, every evening, I stopped to look at the grooves in his face, the bend of his cheekbone, the wave of his hair, the intensity of his stare. And each time, I said *something*. I always said something. "I'm sorry" or "I'm ashamed" or "I'm such a fuck-up" or "Why?" or "What's going to happen?" or "What do you think about all this?" or "This is misery" or "Forgive me" or "Hey" followed by a deep, heavy sigh. The beauty of this painting is that His expression seemed to match my sentiment each time.

Once, during a break I sat there by Him on the floor. There were no audible words; just tears, heavy shame, grief, and loss. His hair blowing in the wind, he remained calm and sweet. I felt comforted, like maybe His imaginary, painted arms reached out and rested on my shoulders as one would do when they are a perfectly-painted, empathetic Deity. I rested there in those imaginary arms and let the worries fall from my eyes into the worry lines in his face.

We sat, and we cried for all that was lost, which, at the time, felt like *everything*. And I do mean everything: divorce looming; custody in peril; job lost; housing in peril; a horribly-dysfunctional romantic attachment with a married man while sitting in rehab for sex addiction. *Surely this was rock bottom.* I laid down there under Jesus' big head with all my big problems and cried and cried and cried. The moments were healing moments, ones I'll never forget.

I expected to meet Jesus at sex camp, but I did not expect my healing to connect directly and so vividly with an amazing piece of art. But that's Jesus, isn't it? Showing up where very few want to go with you, in unexpected ways, at unexpected times, and whose healing is as unique as your issues.

It was all grace, actually.

Who am I? Why am I here?

I'm here because he saw her. They said yes to adulterous passion. It's simple as that.

Eons before all that, He decided to make a Grace Sandra Green. Throughout 1976, He did a little knitting.

He knew my name, frame, and favorite video game: Tetris.

A centennial baby, He said.

That covers the "how," unless we focus on those pesky "whys" that give us these existential mid-life crises.

Who am I after *grit* and grace, *in between* the passionate lover and the angry advocate?

Dunno.

I am lost. I am found.

Grace Sandra

I am slathered in grace but bound by judgement. {My own}
I am quiet with Him. I am loud in emotion.
I am sorry. I am proud.
I am beautiful. I am off-yellow.
I am a Mama. I am selfish.
I am dreaming. I am nightmaring.
I am broken. I am a healer.
I am in the middle.
Keep knitting, God.
Keep knitting.

On April 8, 2015, I read a post from author Anne Lamott on her Facebook page. "All truth is a paradox. Life is a precious unfathomably beautiful gift; and it is impossible here, on the incarnational side of things. It has been a very bad match for those of us who were born extremely sensitive. It is so hard and weird that we wonder if we are being punked." Whenever Anne says something that resonates, I'm encouraged to put a few words down as well. Here's what I wrote that day.

For a couple of days, I've been marinating on something my friend and author Sarah Bessey wrote "Sometimes, the most fearless thing we can do is keep showing up."

Lately on Facebook, I've hinted, hemmed, and hawed about going to Anonymous meetings. I've been clear to never state that I am going to *Sex* Addicts Anonymous and not Alcoholics Anonymous, which is what most assume, and a few have stated as much.

I get it. Even with public failed relationships and marriages, it's easier to assume that I'm addicted to alcohol than sex. To be clear, I'm not addicted to sex. I'm addicted to love. And I'm not trying to be cute either. I am *actually a love addict*. Because love addiction is a smaller subset of people and the ramifications aren't quite as dire, it's not often taken as seriously. The honest truth is that there aren't very many in-person Love Addicts Anonymous meetings in my city. By the by, I attended Sex Addicts Anonymous for a year and a half. It helped me tremendously. Also, when my addiction blew up in my face, it did so with the addition of lots of sex. I knew the meetings couldn't hurt. I'm grateful for each and every one.

I left each meeting more inspired and self-aware than the last. I wish I'd started years and years earlier. I've skirted around writing about the meetings because acknowledging a sex or love addiction struggle felt shameful as a woman. For starters, the fear of being viewed through the lens of "just a hoe" felt too heavy to bear. If even being willing to walk into meetings typically consisting of all men felt scary, you can appreciate and understand why I've danced a jig around the issues publicly.

Addressing all of this, has been painful, painful, painful.

And then shameful, shameful, shameful.
And then fearful, fearful, fearful.
And then hopeful, hopeful, hopeful.
And then painful, painful, painful all over again.
And then the cycle starts over. Rinse. Repeat.
This is the world I'm in now by which I am still surprised.

Grace Sandra

I'm an addict. I struggle with addictions. I go to Anonymous meetings (and they rock). I did a rehab week. It helped. The world kept spinning.

As I gain momentum in sobriety, in understanding my issues, in working through the Twelve Steps, I hope to keep showing up to write-it-out, both publicly and privately. I hope to; I don't know how much I will, but I hope to.

I understand that to barrel through the messy and the beautiful in front of community and surrounded by community is needed. When I think about every word Anne Lamott and Brennan Manning have put down about their experiences as sober, drunk, recovering, sober, drunk, recovering alcoholics in and out of Alcoholics Anonymous, I am deeply indebted to their honesty. I draw strength from their successes and failures as I put pen to paper, even privately.

Some of us who've hit rock bottom never believed we'd *actually* hit rock bottom. I hit it head first. I'm still bleeding out from that head-lacerating experience, concussed at least. There is wisdom in the marination time. I will likely marinate for the rest of my life. I will be in pursuit of healing for the rest of my life.

When deep in addictions, there's always something else lying directly beneath the surface begging to be unearthed, which undoubtedly brings either a) another addiction, b) post-traumatic stress disorder, c) a shit-ton of confusion and pain, or d) all of the above. In my case, d) all of the above, I've had no choice but to walk through this with as many yolk-fellows as possible. One does not simply walk into the eye of the storm alone.

There's a small part of me that wants to fully hide throughout this process. In all the ways I've stayed quiet,

I have already. I could shut down my blog and deactivate Facebook, and I could say it's about refocusing and yada yada yada (not that those are bad things), but there's a part of me that would feel deeply satisfied with that course of action because I am *still rebuilding* from the giant clusterfuck.

There's this other part of me, an even bigger part, that wants to show up and write about it with messages of messy faith and messy hope in and for community.

This other part of me wants to write about it because this is the world I'm in now—remarkably, shockingly, surprisingly.

Another part of me wants to be ballsy enough to tell these stories because why not? They acknowledge that I'm a sinner. These stories acknowledge my humanity. My fallen-ness. My confusion. My stress, depression, or issues.

There's a part of me that knows my stories and my current-day experiences aren't of less value than things I wrote five or six years ago simply because my life was more "put together" those days.

There's a part of me that wants to challenge those who believe that the messy-faith-wrestlers can't and shouldn't have a voice that speaks to God's grace.

So. I've thought about this idea of showing up.

I'm not merely concerned with showing up online. I'm trying to show up at my boys' schools more often, show up for my Anonymous meetings, show up for my workouts, show up to my time with the Lord, show up to consistent work hours, and more of the being-a-grown-up-showing-up-variety.

Of course, there's always other ways I need to work on showing up as well: showing up for counseling; showing up for more reading, less television; showing up for more creativity, less Instagram; and showing up for more self-care, less self-loathing.

For today, I'm showing up here to remember it's okay to show up scared and to acknowledge the fear.

I wrote this in the fall of 2015.

When my first ex-husband and I separated, I took so few things. I didn't want a lot from that house, honestly. Over the years, I'd become completely overwhelmed with more than a decade of pack-rat accumulation. There was so much.

So much stuff.

The mess of that house was the face of our despair. I took my books and my clothes and not much else with the exception a fake plant. Not a coffee table, not a sheet set. Not a couch. Not a fork, not a cup, not a pot to piss or cook in. I started my life post separation in a mostly-empty apartment for which I was incredibly grateful. The emptiness was a reminder of the freedom from *all sorts of messes* I'd been eager to escape.

Loss: 1 of 4

It quickly became apparent that the one thing I had too much of, the one thing that could make even a mostly-empty apartment seem downright filled to capacity, was the ridiculous amount of clothes in my closet. And on the floor of the closet. And next to the bed. And on the floor of the laundry room. And everywhere.

Still. I couldn't get rid of them. Emotionally. Physically. Spiritually. The sadness of the separation made it difficult to do anything, to lose anything else, *anyone else*. Not my jeans, too. *Et tu, Brute?*

The clothes were just the beginning. There was so much more I needed to get rid of, to pare down. *How do you let go of all that is familiar and comforting even as it continues to stress and dismember any semblance of peace?*

It took me over a year, but I ended up donating ten garbage bags full of clothes and jewelry to the Goodwill. The donated shoe count got up to 54 pairs. I still think about some of those clothes. There was one cream, sheer-armed shirt from Target that I lost. There was one really-nice LBD, fitted, warm, and glorious. Both, ironically enough, got left at the house I think. I don't miss most of them at all.

I recently cut more than fourteen inches off my hair.

I was tired of the hair maintenance. I'd always rather spend time snuggling my boys on pizza/movie night or hanging out with my new husband during times I should have been performing the necessary chores in order to keep my big, natural hair healthy.

More than that, I was ready to pare down. I was ready to loose myself from the cultural ideas that my "long, pretty hair" made me a better person or a prettier woman. I wanted a drastic reminder that I'd be okay with less.

Grace Sandra

Less hair.

Moreso, I was bored. I was tired.

Tired of playing with it, tired of spending money on expensive hair products, and bored to smithereens watching YouTube hair tutorials so I could learn how to maintain and style those long locks.

It took me a few months. Other than my husband, I knew very few would support the big chop until after it was done. I tossed and I toiled, but I followed through. I don't feel as pretty or even normal, but it was time to pare back, and it's okay. I am okay. I lost some things.

I lost some hair.

I lost some things that *will* grow back. I'll live.

I lost some things that *won't* grow back. I'll live.

Recently, my new husband and I lost two precious, little babies we desperately wanted and put great effort and planning into conceiving. I had two miscarriages in three weeks. Obviously, those losses weren't intended. I wasn't paring down, by any stretch.

We lost those beloved babies, but we survived, as humans tend to do in the face of our greatest enemy: death.

Today, I mourn the loss of a young man, taken far too young by cancer. His young wife, their young daughter, everyone it seems, is facing life's ultimate paring system. I believe God's grace is sufficient to cover us all in our losses whether we choose to acknowledge, believe, or hope in it.

Masked as our losses are by divorce, stuff, miscarriages, and cancer, loss is loss. Reminders tell us another day has passed without a reasonable solution or explanation. Every loss is tragic.

Also, I pared down my blog way down. Mostly, I'm over myself. For now.

2 of 4

I used to be a Minister. I served in a ministry position for twelve years. For 259 reasons, I walked away from it, which was healthy and necessary at the time, though it made such little sense. I didn't have anything else lined up, but we needed the income, and it had been a dream job I thought I would retire doing. But I left. It is one of the only decisions I've ever made that required me to trust my intuition to bring some things to a needed end even when it wasn't clear exactly why. The stated reason was that I needed a break, as if I were playing a game of basketball and needed a half time.

Intuitively, I knew the storm brewing in my heart and life was bigger than I could handle. At that time, I was one half of a crumbling, toxic marriage. I was at peak dysfunction—primarily by flirting with other men—and awash in horribly dysfunctional conflict. My ex-husband was seeping in codependent behavior. The worse I got, the worse he got. Our cycles were spinning out of control. We'd spent over a decade fine tuning our particular dysfunctions, and they were operating on all cylinders. It's taken me more than five years to understand how we were making each other worse as opposed to me taking full responsibility, not only for myself, but also the state of the marriage. We've both experienced much growth, if you're wondering.

I went on to have a breakdown of sorts including, but not limited to, depression and spectacular moral failures of epic proportions. The marriage disintegrated into a million ugly pieces, followed by a traumatic divorce and an equally-traumatic custody battle in which I genuinely feared I would lose my children for having an affair. During that time, I lost my job, every penny I had, I was nearly homeless, slightly suicidal, and spent a week in sex-addiction rehab, followed by months in Sex Addicts Anonymous meetings. I threw away a lot. I ran from a lot. I lost a lot. I hurt a lot. It was a whole thing.

When I've casually thrown around the phrase "I put a blowtorch to my life," I have not exaggerated. I found myself vague-booking to spare both the reader and myself the immense shame of a somewhat-public fall from glory. I went from being everyone's favorite this-and-that, up-and-coming-this, and look-out-for-her to the absolute rock bottom. I became not just the rock at the bottom, but the mold that grows on the bottom of the rock that lives at Rock Bottom.

I don't even want to know all the things that were said about me during that time. There are friends I assumed would love me all the way through who essentially said,

Loss: 2 of 4

"You're too messy" and "I'm scared of you." I lost many communities and many friends.

As an aside, if one is ever tempted to be jealous of my redemption story, one should rethink the whole notion. I wouldn't wish my trek through hell and back on anyone. Even redemption stories are bathed in the refiner's fire.

One of the many consequences of that perfect storm was that I stopped sharing how my faith directly coincides with my passions. My passion for social justice, racial reconciliation, anti-racism, and my work to be an active voice and participant in dismantling white supremacy and systemic racist practices like police brutality in the judicial system were all disconnected from my faith.

I thought: who on earth wants to hear me talk about my faith or God? Regardless of content, is there a place for me to wed those issues?

In light of my past, my present, or even my future, I knew I simply did not have the same influence I once had. I did not and do not have the leadership I once had, nor have I had the platform, and that needed to be okay. It was okay. It has been okay. I took a seat.

I took a damn seat. I'm edging off that seat, learning to forgive myself, and moving on. But my ass is still in the seat. To be fair, my glutes are engaged. *I am definitely* considering standing all the way up again.

I needed a lot of time to reflect and mourn—roughly five years. I could do with more. I still mourn the heavy losses. My ex-husband and I have talked about these matters ad nauseam. We have debriefed. We have cried together. We have forgiven one another. We have asked many questions. We have answered many questions. We have left 7-minute Voxer messages getting to the bottom of what happened. We have helped one another understand what was happening in each of us when things got really bad. We have become *actually* reconciled and kind co-parents. I'm incredibly grateful for him.

The biggest gift came by helping each other understand that, in a shocking turn of events, it was not about the other person. Each of us were operating from a deep place of pain, and it was not personal. Seventeen years of togetherness (almost all of them married), two kids, two cats, and a home, and it was still not personal. My choices were desperate, grabby, foolhardy attempts at survival. And vice versa.

What's most surprising about us is that all of this understanding has come without any conflict whatsoever. I did not know that was possible for us. Once everything was off the line, once my choices no longer directly impacted him, once we'd each done our inner work, there was space for us to be our true and most honest selves without shame or despair. Which is to say, sometimes, but not all the time, some couples need to get divorced so they can have peace with one another.

Now, things are different. I'm trying to survive something I've never known with 100 percent certainty I'm supposed to survive. If you've ever done something risky or wrong in the name of desperation, or white-knuckled your way through addiction or fear, and made many consecutive, survival-based choices, then you understand a bit of what my life has felt like. A series of break-neck, survival-based choices. When you reach that point, passions and hobbies, even your entire career, seems woefully superfluous.

A distant acquaintance randomly reached out to me with words from the Lord regarding my silence. She told me it was time to start using my voice again. I have never been unwilling, but I have been afraid. Deeply, deathly, shamefully, woefully afraid because I was A Minister of Our Lord And Savior Jesus Christ.

Also, timing is important.

In the meantime, I have not been silent about my passions nor my fierce, mother-bear instincts towards my people; I've just not connected those passions to my faith. I've not connected them to my deeply-held belief that God is a God of justice, that God is the God of Black Americans, or that our vulnerabilities—from police brutality to poverty and everything in between—cause God to mourn.

Then, August 2014 happened. The murder of Mike Brown, protests across the country, racial unrest culminating in the election of Donald Trump for crying out loud. All of it lit a fire in me. It was the fire former Pastor Bill Hybels spoke of as "holy discontent," the area in which God has so emboldened and gifted you to care about that it produces a sense of unquenchable anger or discontent if nothing changes. When it comes to my people, I've felt this holy discontent since I was thirteen. Perhaps younger. Even more, I felt *called* to it.

Yes, called.

I am beginning to allow myself to see past surviving, which gives me the bravery to see a survival and hope. That is the recurring theme of my past decade of written work as it is, but I'd also like to explore living. Perhaps, even, (gasp) thriving.

If I had
   the power of invisibility,
   the power of flight,
   the power of unlimited strength,
   I would unleash a rage
   built up over these years
   settling on tired shoulders.
   A rage like this world has never seen.
   Rage at my father.
   Rage for little girls, cut.
   Rage for my people.
   Rage at the powerful.
   Rage at the lawmakers.
   Rage at the suits.
   Rage for black women.

Rage for sex slavery.
Rage at his betrayal.
Rage at his narcissistic abuse.
Rage for Kalief Browder.
Rage for beaten dogs.
Rage for colonization.
Rage for my city.
Rage.
Rage here,
Rage there,
Rage everywhere,
and there would be no end.
While the heavens cry out the glory of God,
my reign of terror
would barely be satiated
by death's sting
at murderous hands.
But I have no power
of invisibility,
of flight,
of unlimited strength.
No platform.
No flight.
No fight.
No strength.
No money.
No home.
No respect.
No husband.
Nothing to brag or boast.
There is no power to speak of
but this muffled voice
which boasts of my rage

Grace Sandra

and asks who'd I'd be
if I became powerful me.
Let the heavens declare
the glory of His name;
meanwhile, I'll thank God
I have no power to rage,
only desire to make known.
I'll raise my muffled
voice on behalf of those
powerless to use their own.

A reflection I posted to my blog a few days after Thanksgiving, 2016.

The day after Thanksgiving, I sat and cried with my husband about how much I hate Thanksgiving. This year, I find myself emotionally gutted over 45's politics, of course.

My heart was heavy with the deplorable treatment of the Standing Rock protesters attacked with frigid water, in frigid temperatures. Why can't the United States keep its treaties with Native Americans? Why are we incapable of treating Native Americans fairly? *Why, God, why?* My heart hurts for them. They fight to protect sacred land and are nearly killed for doing so.

So. There's that. Sigh.

Grace Sandra

Without fail, every year I tend to dread Thanksgiving and Christmas. Has anyone else noticed the incredible expectations attached to these days? You and your big, beautiful family must all be happy, thankful, and full on Pinterest-worthy cuisine.

Insert eye-roll emoji. These expectations were something I read loud and clear long before social media gave us clues about not only what we should *feel* on these holidays, but what it should *look* like as well. The feast of unending, jealous longing and useless comparisons as grand as the 20-pound turkey spread on the table.

The failed expectations of life with a happy family is a simplified version of my issues, and really, only the tip of the iceberg. I imagine all of us feel that way to an extent, right? We're all *trying to be thankful*—despite, perhaps, many deep layers of pain—not only because it's almost the only socially-acceptable attitude on Thanksgiving, but because what kind of uncouth heretic can't find a way to express gratitude one day of the year, no less, a day supposedly set aside to cultivate thankfulness?

The pain for me is always about belonging. Isn't it always for everybody?

Aren't we always asking...

Where do I belong?
Do I belong here?
Do I fit here?
Do they want me here?
Am I home here?
If not here, where?
Where do I belong?

For most of us from broken homes, the endless questions of belonging are heightened during the holidays.

I don't remember the year, nor my age, but I was fairly young when I started feeling the oppressive weight of depression on Thanksgiving. A large part was due to the absence of my Dad and my inability to connect with his family. He left for prison when I was eleven. The subsequent hole gutted me emotionally on many occasions, of course, but holidays held a peculiar and specific sting. I could have never articulated that as a kid. Hell, I barely knew how to engage emotional pain at all. That little girl definitely didn't understand what made her sadness linger like such a distracting nuisance as she ate her apple pie.

The other confusing dynamic was the slow nag of being racially and culturally different from everyone else no matter whose house I was in. Growing up biracial meant when I was with my Ma's side, there were white folks present all the time. When I was with my Dad's side, there were black folks present all the time.

Before my Dad's imprisonment, my access to him and his family was limited. I understood the finality of his lock-up to mean certain death of those relationships. There was no going back. On Thanksgiving, I longed for him and his family which felt forever lost to me and for me.

Thanksgiving feels like displacement.

In my early adulthood, my Ma still made a big meal and invited me, my siblings and her grandkids over. When her paranoid schizophrenia got worse, she lost her house, my childhood home, after 25 years of home ownership. The loss was the last bit of normalcy our core family would ever experience together. From then on,

Grace Sandra

Thanksgiving location and hosting was up in the air. I tried to host one time. I could try to explain why that experience stressed me the junk out, but I'll leave it at this: I'm no natural hostess. At all.

For many Thanksgivings, my ex-husband and I bounced around from his parents' house, my sister's house, my best friend's house, the homes of mutual co-workers, or anyone who'd have us. As welcome as we were, year-after-year the longing for my "normal" family, for a familiar place, for racial and cultural belonging or understanding eluded me. The thought of it sat like an elephant on my chest with so much dead weight. On Thanksgiving, the elephant moves around, gets cozy, and snuggles up. I can't breathe.

Post divorce, an additional painful layer joined the club. Alternating Thanksgiving with my two precious boys meant spending a major holiday without even seeing them, let along building annual traditions. This at first seemed impossible. It became manageable, of course, but this new dynamic is what threw me over the top in the final death blow of utterly hating Thanksgiving.

I can't get out of my feelings. I can't "thank away" my grief. I can't overlook the oppressive sense of loss. I can't deny the brokenness of my entire family. I can't whisk away the feelings that I don't belong. I can't ignore the jealousy towards put-together families splashed across timelines, and I can't lay aside fears that whoever I'm with on Thanksgiving won't also one day toss me aside like yesterday's trash.

I hate Thanksgiving. It takes two days, sometimes three, to regain emotional equilibrium.

I'll never hermit myself. I'll always go, always participate. Always look, long, and lunge for hope. I'll always pray for peace. Always cultivate gratitude. But it will likely remain a day with pain.

That's okay.

A meager request.
I pray my sons will grow up to become the first two men in my life I don't have to survive.

Chase me.

My precious husband and my best friend. Your love gives me a renewed passion and zest for life.

Everyday I wake up with the awareness that you are my husband, and my heart is filled with joy. You are my husband, and very little has meant more to me than that.

On the beach, I peered into your soul while the Holy Spirit blew my hair.

With God present, I promised to have and hold you, my Love. I said, "I do," and I would do it all over again. I want little else in the world but for your love to pursue me, day in and day out.

Take me, My Love, and hold me forever. Love me day in, day out. Choose me, everyday. Pursue me. Chase after

Love: 2 of 6

my mind, my heart, my body. I long for your pursuit as strongly as gravity pulls my body to the earth. Chase me!

My heart pulls towards yours like the earth is pulled to twist and turn on its navigational path. The beat quickens at the sound of your voice and the moments we spend entangled in embrace, the slowest kisses in between each heavy breath.

I think of your fingers slowly moving up and down and around, and I long for you. I long for you to reach out your hand to caress my back, my side, my leg. It's magic. My blood courses a bit faster. Ignition. Your touch reverberates throughout me, sending happy hormones to my brain and pleasure elsewhere.

A warm river ebbs and flows to welcome you into my being. You come inside, My Love, cum in here where you and I are safe. I am one with you in spirit.

My body melts into your persona, and it feels as if we've never been apart. You are mine fully, and the gratitude jerks and shrieks out of me, uncontrollably. In the safety, I moan. I breathe in your scent deeply, and it fills me head to toe. Your presence alone stands in distinction. With you, I am me. I am seen. I am free to love, to protect, to serve.

You are safe, My Love. With me, you will never wonder if you are truly seen, truly loved, truly adored.

With me, My Love, you will never be without a partner who treasures your gifts and sees every flaw, who chooses to not only embrace, but celebrate, each joy and pain which accompany each gift and flaw.

Take me, My Love, and hold me forever. Love me day in, day out. Choose me. Pursue me. Chase after my mind, my heart, my body. I long for your pursuit as strongly as gravity pulls my body to the earth. Chase me!

Come to me, My Love. I miss you.

I love his hands.
   They are

   Soft
   Firm
   Warm
   Strong
   Big
   Safe

   I love when
   they slide back and forth across my torso
   I love when
   they squeeze the meaty backside of my rump
   I love when

Love: 3 of 6

they angle up and down my back
I love when
they reach for me, to search for my skin

I love when
they go up my shirt to find their familiar friends
I love when
they go down looking for buried treasure
When the soft, firm, warm, strong hands caress me
I love when
I'm in heaven

This morning I woke up afraid. There was a bit of a thunderstorm, and the slow rumble while I slept jerked me awake in fear of an earthquake. Earthquakes are incredibly rare where I live, but the accompanying fear was present despite its unrealistic origin. Instead of being able to roll over and go back to sleep, the fear latched on to other things, as it almost always does because gripping fear is a miserable shrew.

    I wanted to hold my husband, desperate to be covered by him like a Mama bird engulfing her chick in her wings. I find complete safety in his embrace, particularly in the morning, providing me that extra courage typical from intimate, human connection. But he's not here this morning, and I feel the loss of his physical presence acutely. In the very next moment, I'm overcome with gratitude for his friendship, and I know in the next few days he'll be home. My love will be home, and my anticipation momentarily calms.

Yet, the fear of my waking moments coupled with overwhelming appreciation for my husband expresses itself in a groaning prayer: *God, my God, my God!* I bring it all to Him. I'm reminded as I've been prone to lately, how I'm hurting over the wounds of a friend. I've been trying to let the demise of this friendship—and all that was said—go. How do I bind up the wound, extend forgiveness, truly extending peace and blessing over her life? *God, it hurts.* In the next moment, I remember I've hurt her, too. My mind quickly generates a quick list of at least seven people I've personally hurt in all this. *God, you know my heart, my brokenness, my intentions, my every thought. You know. YOU know, God...my innermost...I didn't mean...*

I pray for a while longer. It's debilitating. Facing the pain others have inflicted on you is one monster to stare down. Facing the pain you've caused others is an entirely different monster with sharper teeth and worse breath.

But I allowed the pain this morning because I know I have to. I cannot run from any of this. But God, I get whiny like a child, *even if all this pain could be taken away tomorrow, what about...*

...earthquakes?
...car accidents?
...breast cancer?
...heart attacks?
...school shootings?
...my kids? my husband?

My God, my God! How do I manage this life down here?! I'm just a speck.

Grace Sandra

I roll over again to my husband's side of the bed where he is not, and I long for him again because he is safety encapsulated in a human body, and I haven't felt spiritually, emotionally, physically safe like this since, maybe, 2008.

I hear little footsteps heading toward the fridge for yogurt sticks with yellow minions on the front. I look at the clock. It's 6:21 a.m., and it's time to face this day which seems to have gotten off on the wrong foot: fear and anxiety and longing. I'm up earlier than normal so I make my coffee and open up the Bible to Psalm 90. I'm particularly comforted by verses 14 and 15:

Surprise us with love at daybreak;
  then we'll skip and dance all the day long.
Make up for the bad times with some good times;
  we've seen enough evil to last a lifetime.
-Psalms 90:14-15, The Message

I make a mental note to text it to my husband later today. I muse that I'm an awesome wife, and I know he actually believes this to be true. (If I can't pull off being an awesome wife in three weeks of marriage, there's a problem. I digress). These verses feel so meaningful in lieu of last night's FaceTime. We'd shared more in depth the evil we've lived through. A few of his stories are heart wrenching, perhaps leading to this morning's awareness of the certainty of life's tragedies.

Yesterday, before all this, I was wildly on top of the world. As a result I felt optimistic and empowered about addressing everything life throws at me—from debt to death and all that is between. I even cleaned out my car, a feat which only happens when hope is present. Today is different. The fears of the unknown and the pain of the past have me emotionally haggard.

    I have an idea: I should write.

If I am love...
I deserve to be loved, cherished, honored, and respected

You love, but do not cherish
I know you don't know how

You provide, but do not respect
I know you don't know how

But is that good enough for me?
I've let you disrespect me
Out of fear
Fear you'd leave
Fear you'd find me too angry

Love: 5 of 6

Fear of your response
Fear of your fragile ego
Fear of your cutting words which have destroyed my soul more than once

And so I let you
Gave consent to my mistreatment
I made you believe it's golden
Because I knew you don't know
any other way

I made excuses for you
So that I wouldn't have to address myself
He doesn't know what he's doing, so forgive

I made excuses for me
So that I wouldn't have to face the coward I've been

Too afraid to demand that you love me through respect
But mostly too afraid to love myself

Could you learn how to love me?
Could I learn to love me?

And now here we are
Our lives inextricably bound up together by new life
And I wish I never met you

I have loved you
But you have left me

If you came back to me

Grace Sandra

Even if you didn't know how
I'd take you in
And wrap my legs around you

Because I still do not love me
I still do not love me enough for the both of us.

Many days, it's awful being an empath. Being a broken empath? Nearly unbearable. As I understand it, I have been given the "gift" of empathy. Before I was old enough to cultivate it, God set it down on my lap and said, Here have this. You will weep for others.

When people first started to connect with my writing, they kept telling me it was my empathy that drew them in. This was long before I'd ever done any serious inquiry into the life of an empath. Certainly nothing that may have protected me. You have a gift, they'd say. You should write more vulnerable stuff, they'd say. All right, I Kanye shrugged. No biggie.

But empathy is the taking on of others' pain. And I am a "high empath." Whether I'm invested in a person or people group or country or not, I am feeling their pain almost as if I were living their lives. When I am closely connected to someone's pain unleashed in irresponsible ways, I am absorbing their toxicity much like the dude on Heroes who absorbed others' powers after he killed them. Except I don't kill people, so there's that.

My husband and I talked through each traumatizing event of 2016 that he put me through. Here was our attempt at healing. There were 12. One in each month, minimum. The can of worms was opened wide, and each day they slithered through my soul with no attempt at exit. The process left me soul weary. At the time, I was the primary emotional support to a dear friend I love, who was being hunted by her ex-husband. I felt anguish for her unrelenting fear. The empathy felt heavy. Too heavy. Another of my best friends was in the throes of major depression. A few days after that, my brother's fiancé told me he was back in jail.

I was at a grief limit. I couldn't listen to or engage in anything even remotely abusive or toxic. I was slowly absorbing verbal violence from my husband, busy at work to repair him like a worker bee serving it's Queen. I could not engage in any sort of "othering" comments or articles.

I could not watch television with violence, racism, rape, or murder. I felt frequently disturbed. I had (and still have) nightmares. I began to develop Post Traumatic Stress Disorder. I was going through something I had never experienced in my adult life in a pressure-cooker-like state. I tried to tell people I was suffering without explicitly saying, "I am being abused." Everyone told

Love: 6 of 6

me, You are an empath; just keep writing. Things will get better. He will get better.

It is helpful for me to remind myself of this often: a lot of people are suffering a lot of the time. We grow weary of their suffering, and we mute them on Instagram and Facebook at best: at worst, we unfriend, unfollow, and block them. We don't ask people the honest questions and don't care to invest in the deeper stories, even when there are tears or symptomatic behavior. Many of us are heavy-enough social-media users it can seem as if most people are not suffering, hardly ever. We would do well to remember that this is not true.

My friend Tonia asked me what I thought of these endlessly-optimistic-social-media posters. Perhaps, I muse, these people's lives are falling apart. Maybe they are trying like hell to forge beauty, gratitude, and optimism among the tragedy of endless dysfunction and fuckery.

I fail often, but I try to remind myself of the humanity of imperfect people. My imperfect humanity is wrapped up in greed, lust, and laziness to name a few, but empathy tethers me to mercy for others even when—perhaps especially when—I'm a judgmental asshole.

There were times when the sense of joy I had for my children felt complete. Final. As if nothing could steal it away. On other days that year, I wept with the Lord deep, fat, angry tears of grief. I prayed for the finality of death to come snatch me out of this life. *In an act of mercy, Lord, just let me go.*

In an act of mercy.

An hour later, I'd see my daughter smile. As if by some miracle, I'd feel ready to engage the world again with heavily-filtered photos uploaded to Instagram. Look at her smile, I'd say. Isn't this worth everything in the world? Hashtag Gratitude. Hashtag blessed. Hashtag MomLife. I'd feel courage to keep going for four hours until after the evening baths when despair would grab hold again. This is humanity at our best and worst. We fight for survival yet it doesn't ever feel like courage and barely lasts past dinnertime.

Except when it does.

One of my best friends, Jean always tells me to take things one day at a time. This time frame could be reduced to one hour or one minute depending on the destitution of the circumstances. This advice once seemed trite until I lived in a scenario which necessitated a need to take it.

Deep down, I knew that my hunted friend, my depressed friend, and I were bad ass.

We're all minority women, all biracial. White with Lebanese; white with Black; white with Brazilian. All of us with fucked-up childhoods and equally fucked-up parents. All of us have endured toxic and abusive marriages. All of us have survived adulting tomfoolery.

Still, here we are. Surviving and junk. Pushing through. Waking up each day. Taking good care of our babies (seven between us). Here we are making bold and courageous decisions with fear in our bellies. Here we are with Master's degrees. I am proud of us. And maybe you would be, too. If you knew what we've been through, you would be.

When I walked with them, I realized how undeniable their strength is. When applied to me, the assurance was slow to come. I was afraid to see myself that way. Everyone has seemed so comfortable squeezing into the little box of empathy and pain. There is Grace. She's the little broken one. For many years, I was comfortable owning

Love: 6 of 6

that. It kept me playing small. I could hide. I could be lazy; there was not much expectation.

When I realized I was enduring humiliating psychological abuse every single day, everything changed. When I began to share with trusted peers exactly what was happening, I saw how their perception of me changed, too. They told me I was strong. I watched their horrified faces turn to compassion, and I knew only a strong woman could endure this and get up every day to fight for her freedom again. Today, I have zero doubt in my mind the strength that's buried deep in these yellow bones. No doubt at all.

My empathy began extending out to grab not only the pain of my sisters (as usual), but for the first time, courage and strength began to flow from their veins to mine, from my veins to theirs. When I began to value my own strength, empathy became less of a pain exchange. Once I learned to harness my boundaries against toxic people, I could enjoy the beauty in connection born of vulnerability.

More than anything, I wanted to survive even though every day I woke up feeling that I probably would not. I feared I would not survive my husband, staying or leaving him. I feared I would lose my children. Somehow, their fathers would find a way and remove them from me. I feared my depression and anxiety would consume me. I feared suicide.

The fears were mighty, but I never stopped fighting for survival. I didn't want to betray the words I'd had tatted on my hand several years earlier, "Always hope."

I still posted to Instagram. I posted selfies and images of my children. I tried to show that my life was more than my abuse and that I had reasons to have joy. Sometimes

Grace Sandra

I posted out very obvious cries for help, hoping someone would notice and ask me if they could help me escape. The incongruence of my posts squelched any narrative which implied I was in trouble. Every day I woke up wanting to survive, and my social media accounts felt like an accurate representation of that desire.

Life is always more complex than a curated life on the 'gram. Hopefully we all know that by now.

Now go be a human. Find gratitude. Be inspired. Survive. Love someone well. Forgive yourself. Pray.

This present moment is all we have.

It was Valentine's Day. I sent my husband out to get a vegan pizza and salted caramel cashew ice cream. It had been a rough day, and I desperately wanted the comfort. It had been a "gone day," marked by PMDD. A gone day feels like insomnia, being barely being able to get out of bed, perpetually furrowed brows, and such little motivation to survive that staying upright and feeding yourself feels monumental.

PMDD, premenstrual dysphoric disorder is like PMS, but if PMS were on heroin. It shows up about a week before your cycle, lasting until it starts or soon after. PMDD produces mood swings, extreme depression and feelings of hopelessness, intense anger and desire for conflict, tension, anxiety, irritability, difficulty concentrating, fatigue, loss of appetite, feeling out of control, trouble sleeping, headaches, and more.

For me, PMDD presents as extreme depression and hopelessness, high anxiety, and suicidal ideations. I have no desire to read or watch television or even distract myself. I do not enjoy playing with or engaging my children, and it feels awful to do anything but hide my face. On the worst days, I don't want to do anything but lie in bed, even if I'm not sleeping. PMDD gets very intense for me.

It has varied in intensity surrounding the births of my children and the fiasco childbirth has on women's hormones. I've experienced PMDD for up to ten days before my cycle to a more reasonable one-to-three days before. Then, my cycle will begin, and magically, it's if God himself turned off the switch for Grace's PMDD symptoms to end. Just like that—poof—it's gone. I get back to loving to read, to watching a bit too much television, to distracting myself on Instagram, to playing with my kids, and trying but mostly failing to cook healthy food that all of them will actually eat.

After the Gone Days, when things go back to normal, I am left feeling grateful for the reprieve, but also a bit crazy. The switch from intense feelings of hopelessness to a laissez-faire, hunky-dory existence makes you question your overall sanity.

Can I just scratch the record for one moment to remind us all what an amazing joy it is to be a woman?

While my husband was out procuring said vegan treats, I came across a TED talk describing how childhood trauma affects health for a lifetime. I wailed and wailed. As one does. The speaker went into depth about ACE scores, a predictor of the severity of childhood trauma.

Grace Sandra

ACE stands for Adverse Childhood Experiences, and its scores tally different types of abuse and neglect of a childhood marked by trauma. The higher your score, the more at risk you are for health problems later in life.

My ACE score is a 7. It's a less-than-hopeful score. On this day, I did not feel shocked or shaken; I had taken it before. I knew I was doomed. Besides all the other ramifications for adult survivors of severe childhood trauma, an early death expectancy wasn't any shock, either.

As a little girl, I spent time worrying about having a shorter life; that was my lot. I wasn't a creepy kid obsessed with death, either. My assumption was that I'd never survive my father's sexual abuse. I thought he would give me A.I.D.S., and I'd die before high school. I wasn't certain I would survive my brother. His constant verbal and emotional abuse, his out of control rage, and violent outbursts left me certain I'd die at his hands sooner or later. I carried a heavy burden for the cardinal sin of being born even half-black in America that I assumed would kill me if my father or brother couldn't finish the job.

The way trauma affected me as a kid was to fill my little heart with pervading hopelessness day in and day out. I carried burdens far too heavy for one kid to worry about. I kept them inside for years on end as if it were my job.

I'd experienced so much covert and overt racism from my white church, my mostly-white private school, and even my own white family members that I didn't know there were white people *who weren't racist*. The idea that white people exist who are actively anti-racist was something I couldn't conceptualize. By twelve years old, I didn't know there was a reality in which *I'd ever be treated like an actual human being* by white people. Not ever.

By fourteen, I spent an abnormal amount of time wondering what man would eventually kill me. Most of all, I wondered when I'd kill myself. 16? 26? 36? Depression became a huge battle that kicked into high gear shortly after I became sexually active. Choosing sex at fourteen years old marred my soul in a significantly-destructive way.

My father's abuse spanned six years that I can remember, ending when I was eleven, when he was tried, convicted, and sent to prison for the crime. There was barely any time for my little body to recover before I opened myself up for yet another man to take what he wanted. He did not rape me, but it was eight months of sex I never wanted to have. Eight months of sex that mostly hurt, that I did not enjoy, and in which I did not have any orgasms. Maybe one, I think. It's arguable.

I was fourteen, just a baby. A little girl child with no boobs and zero body autonomy. I had no voice whatsoever and gave my hurting body freely to a little boy, not yet a man, doing what I assumed he thought was his right. Between my father and him, by the time I'd wrapped up my fourteenth year of existence, I'd had a lot of sex. I needed time to not be having sex.

When I add up the combination of my fears and lack of safe spaces, it is not surprising that I wanted to die.

It is also not surprising that I grew up to face issues with love and sex addiction. This whole sex thing does not seem to be working out in my favor. Low key. I am still hoping one day it will.

Then, there was witnessing the death of others. I'd seen a few boys from the hood head off to prison for the smallest of infractions. Before my eighteenth birthday, I knew of at least five kids murdered or killed in their teens. One was killed by the cops during a home burglary, one girl was shot point-blank in the head by her boyfriend, and one kid drowned after falling out of a canoe. I knew two kids killed by rival gangs.

It felt pointless and helpless to be a little, black girl because it was. I refuse to gaslight the feelings of my young self. Little Gracie Green mattered. But even then, I did not sugarcoat the troubles of my youth. I told myself the truth with vivid, radical acceptance: life is hard, black folks are suffering, I deserve better, racism is real, and other descriptive, yet honest sentiments I scribbled in endless journals.

If I had space to discuss what I knew of the world, I might have learned skills to cope before my life careened out of control. But I didn't have the spaces. I had no idea how to articulate how desperately mistreated and undervalued I constantly felt by white people. There was no Twitter, Facebook groups, or Tumblr to commiserate. Before the internet, little, black teens growing up in white families experienced isolation unknown to the current generation. Anyone to whom I even remotely insinuated what I was experiencing would gaslight me immediately. This, too, read as oppressive, but what could I do?

It became obvious I wasn't allowed to share my truth nor trust my intuition. It made too many people, much too uncomfortable. I was groomed to be a respectful negro, a quiet negro, a negro who does not stir the pot.

I decided to take that pot and shove it up whoever's ass I could. Long before there was Colin Kaepernick, there was little Gracie Green refusing to put my hand on my heart and recite "The Pledge of Allegiance" to the

American flag, which we were supposed to recite every, single, goddamn morning before school started at my oppressively-racist, white, Christian school. I was divvied out detention and loss of recess and whatever else Mr. Hammond, my 6th grade teacher, could dole out. He held the greatest number of micro-aggressions in a single year that I'd experience in my entire time at that school.

My life as a poor kid, as a black kid, a kid with a father and brother in prison, as a girl, seemed acutely vulnerable, and it was obvious my humanity held such little value in the grand scheme of things.

Little, black girls don't grow up with constant messages of value and worth like little white girls do from our society unless explicitly told and explicitly parented with intentionality. I was not. An early death seemed inevitable. I didn't worry about it a lot; in fact, it all seemed very ho-hum. Another day, another black kid dies. Life goes on.

It wasn't until I began writing in earnest that I realized how unhealthy my earliest perceptions were. How invasive my thoughts were. I've experienced debilitating, depressive episodes with suicidal ideations at least twice a year for twenty years. Twenty years, y'all. This is no small thing.

After that long, the dysfunctional thinking normalizes even as the persistence of my life continues to prove the lies wrong.

I am forty-two. I have fought for my survival at every turn, regardless of my fears. I am proud of myself.

Then, 2016 happened. I was severely traumatized. I was abused. I am still healing. Again, depression and PTSD fell over my life like a heavy, oppressive blanket, and my childhood assumptions came racing back: I will probably not survive this. At one point, I was certain I would not survive the trauma. When I consider my future, I am not confident I could survive another trauma. I wish I could hold more optimism. I spent the next few years in active, thoughtful, engaged recovery while still battling ongoing cycles of abuse. I am healing, but I am also significantly triggered. Even without triggers, CPTSD comes like a thief in the night.

When I woke up on this particular Valentine's Day, I remembered everything from the younger days to present, and I was crushed to the depths. I told myself living was futile. I said, "Just die already and enter your rest. Please." I decided instead of dying that day I'd watch a TED talk. I also watched an episode of "This Is Us." *What could I have possibly been thinking?*

I knew I was in the midst of rehauling my entire way of doing life so that I could survive while facing the statistical reality that I probably would not.

Also? Fuck statistics. I'm still here, ain't I? All is not well. I still wrestle with PMDD. I still have Gone Days. My second husband and I are separated. We will divorce. Our marriage left me weak, ill, traumatized and terrified. I'm still healing from CPTSD. I'm in therapy. I have no happy, Hollywood ending for you; only that I know God is bigger than statistics. I doubt myself too often, but I rarely doubt God's penchant for the miraculous. I know this because on many days I feel mostly normal. I'm still writing. I hold every aspect of my life with deep, abiding gratitude. I feel peace that passes understanding on some of my worst days, but not all. I focus on gratitude like it's the air I breathe. I write out gratitude lists every day in my Miracle Morning routines.

Our kids are all healthy, beautiful, and shockingly normal. It is all God's grace. All confusing. All magical. All amazing. Sometimes, all laced with sorrows upon sorrows.

But here I am. Still alive. Still facing it. My life is a prayer and a testament to redemption and hope. Maybe I'll die young. But it won't be from suicide.

Are you okay?
  They see you cry.
  They see you fall in a fast, steep crumble.
Are you okay?
  There's so much to fear, so much to worry about.
  They roll up their sleeves: what can be done?
Is it going to be okay?
  Dunno, you say.

Maybe not.
Maybe it will hurt for an extraordinarily-long time.
Maybe always.

What happened to you? How did you get...this way?
You know what happened to me.

You know what...he did.
I'm reeling, you cry.
I am reeling.

Why is that so hard to understand? Must they live it to "get it?"
I guess so.
Even I don't fully understand.
Even I.

One day, everything feels like normal should.
The next, shit blows up.
Only difference between the days? Exploration.

Fragile dynamics are explored with unguarded abandon.
It's time to clean shit up, they say. Take stock. Get on with your life. Quit falling back on it.
How does a little girl process her Daddy having sex with her?

Perhaps *she* doesn't...
...but her adult self does.
A little exploration causes not a little havoc.

This looks to me like classic Post Traumatic Stress Disorder, the Dr. says.

Really?
Twenty years later?
How is that even possible?

I am symptomatic.

Grace Sandra

I am nightmaring.
I am reeling.
It is *all* crumbing.

No, I can't pull it together.
No, I can't see.
No, I can't right.
No, you can't fix.
No, you can't change.
No, I can't make you proud.
No, I don't do light-hearted.
Just no.

Yes, I'm escaping.
Yes, I'm distracting.
Yes, I'm anesthetizing.

This time.
All of *this?*
It has to be.
There is no other way.
Face forward.
Stare it down.
Go with or without.

I am not your fun friend anymore.
I am not put together anymore.
I have nothing to offer you anymore.
I have nothing.

Yes, I'm wandering.
No, I'm not okay.
Yes, I am sorry.

You don't have to leave.
You don't have to judge.
You don't have to have lived it.
You don't have to understand.
You don't have to "get it."
You don't have to *anything at all*…but love.

Love.
Grace.
Compassion.
Mercy.
Tiny modicums of understanding.
Base-level empathy.

Because…
I am not okay.
Not even a little bit.
I rest in Him.
You rest in complexity.
Rest.

I was jittery nervous in that witness box. I shoved sweaty hands under my little thighs to keep them from shaking. Across and in front of me, Ma was on my left, Dad on my right. On my direct right, the honorable Judge So-And-So presiding. The court recorder was down in front. The jury, my lawyer, my father's lawyer, and a room full of strangers were watching the proceedings. I was not briefed beforehand. Though vague memories of "Just be honest, honey," persist.

Questioning began. My lawyer asked questions, and I answered politely. I got a warm reception. Then, he asked me to use my fingers to describe what my Dad had done. I said no. I looked to my father, but he wouldn't make eye contact.

He was understandably mortified, but I was, too. I needed him to look at me. I didn't move for what felt like a long time. I had the feeling of dread coursing through my body. You know the feeling you get when your car starts slipping and you're certain you're going to plunge into dark, icy waters and die a frightful death? It was like that. It was an adrenaline-pumping, stomach-turning, hand-shaking, dry-mouth extravaganza. I looked to Ma for reassurance. Her face revealed anxiety, redness, fear, and disgrace. I looked to the Judge, who looked impatient.

I realized I didn't have anyone to look to survive the events of the day.

I considered running out as fast as I could only I wasn't sure what would happen to me. I literally didn't know if the day would end with *me being shuffled off to prison*. Perhaps in one of the most fearful moments of my life: I showed him. In front of the entire courtroom. I used my fingers to show them all what he had done. I was alone.

I *thought* I was alone.

My lawyer continued to question me in the most polite way he could muster: "Yes, thank you and then what did he do?" "Yes, thank you and then what happened?" "Uh-huh, okay, and then what did he say?"

He asked uncomfortable questions with an uncomfortable look on his face. Questions like "What did Mr. Green do after that?" followed by "And what next?" Stone cold and emotionless, I answered the man.

I looked out to see not only my mother but other women in the stands crying, sniffling, and looking at me with eyes that communicated they had loved me for all of their lives. And they were all Black-American. I was thankful for that, for that solace of not being the minority in this big sterile, wooden room. One woman in the front row looked at me with such care it felt like she could have been right there next to me holding my hand. Through her tears she communicated such sorrow over my answers.

She cried what I was unable to. I think she was my angel, actually. God gave me thirty weeping, loving, black mothers that day. They were God's presence to me. They were the compassion that I needed to answer honestly which ultimately allowed justice to be served. If I could meet them again, I would fall to my knees in gratitude for giving me the strength I simply could not muster without them. The Lord knew I needed that strength for what came next.

My father's lawyer *interrogated* me. He asked leading questions. He asked if I wanted it. Yeah, Mr. Man-of-the-Year asked a child if she *wanted* to be sexually abused by her father. I had faced this trauma with laughter. I'd already gotten quite a few laughs since he began. I answered his asinine question by suggesting we take a poll about how many present would have enjoyed what I went through. I got another uncomfortable laugh. It seemed I was always one step ahead, longing, seeking out those laughs, that approval. When it was time for a break, though, his suggestions set in and squished me. He'd painted me as a horny, lying, sexually-manipulative ten year old. Awesome.

My lawyer and I went to a small, private room for the break. He got all the way down to my eye level. I remember this because he had piercing blue eyes filled with heaviness. "I'm proud of you, Gracie," he said. "You did so well, you did so well," he repeated. "He tried to blame me?" I asked. He hugged me. "I know, I know, but don't you believe him; he has a job to do. It is not your fault! Do you know that?"

I didn't know. I thought *maybe it had been my fault,* and now my father's lawyer cemented it in my brain for the next 20 years. He went on, "Your father made horrible choices, and they are not your choices." I said nothing. He continued, "Lawyer So-And-So...he's a... bastard...he has to do that. He has to ask those questions. You believe me, right?" "Yes," I lied as I noted that "bastard" was a bad word.

It was time for my father to testify. I was led to a quaint room with a security guard while my father attempted to lie his way out of prison. I looked up at the security guard. He winked. The room was a rectangle shape with a large, cherrywood, rectangle-shape table adorning the middle. It had eight fancy, padded chairs around it which the guard gestured to casually as if he preferred me to sit. He stood remarkably still just to the right of the door, staring stiffly ahead.

Ma looked at me reassuringly as she left whispering I'd "be okay" and she'd be "back soon." The lawyer authoritatively warned my guard, "no one in, no one out!" "Yes, sir!" As soon as Ma left, my hands got shaky... again. I paced the room looking at all the ugly decorations: framed paintings of ducks and geese, lamps from 1492, a navy blue and burgundy patterned rug with hints of gold, which were *meant* to comfort, I suppose.

I hugged myself, rocking on the floor. I looked out the window. I clicked my fingernails on the table. I saw something underneath the table. I wondered how many chairs I could cover if I laid across them with my arms stretched all the way out. I flipped over and noticed the dusty underbelly of the table.

He broke the ice. "Are you alright, baby girl?" I crawled out from under the table and looked at him. He was no longer my security detail; he was my friend. "No," I said, "I'm scared." He suggested I sit on the couch and rest. I hadn't noticed a couch. Until he called me "baby girl," I hadn't really noticed him. When a black man calls you "baby girl," it is generally a strong term of endearment communicating friendship, affection, and acceptance. It was as if he took a key and unlocked my box of safety. The safe flew open and all of a sudden, peace filled the room.

He was a good 300 pounds; a 6-foot, 3-inches giant to my barely 70 pounds, 4-foot, 10-year-old self. He was dark-skinned with a sweet face and a gentle disposition. He looked like Ruben Studdard, the velvet teddy bear himself. I asked him to sit on the couch with me, but he couldn't. I understood but cried any old ways. It must have killed my gentle giant.

I wanted him to sit on the couch and invite me onto his lap. I wanted to pull my knees into my chest and fold myself onto his Santa Claus belly. I wanted him to wrap his arms around me and hide my face from the trauma swirling outside the room. I wanted him to pat my ankles and tell me it would be okay. He read my disappointment. He said "I know it's hard what you're going through, but you'll make it. I saw you on that stand. You're going to be an entertainer, ya hear? You'll make it through this. I know you will." With relaxed shoulders, he smiled again. I laid down on the couch. About thirty years later, the door opened, and he stiffened like a board, eyes straight forward, no smile, no indication he'd spoken life to me or called me "baby girl."

Our secret was safe with me.

As I've reflected on the events of this day, I can't figure out if it was one of the worst days of my life or one of the most important.

At worst, I believed the abuse was my fault for twenty years, sent my own Dad off to prison, watched him glare at me as he was carted off in cuffs, and did not see him for another 9 years.

Most importantly, I didn't see my Dad for another 9 years, my abuse ended, justice was served, I found my voice, and I was surrounded by my people who cared for me so remarkably, so distinctively. So importantly.

Also, I realized that day I could make people laugh, really laugh…while being interrogated…while in court…while testifying about my own sexual abuse…at age ten! Priceless.

Most days, I lean towards…important. It's important to remember that God saw fit to care for me through Ma, through these strangers, even through the Detroit court system. It's important for me to remember that I didn't call on God, I didn't pray to God that day, nor did I even consider God that day. On that day, Jesus was not in my vocabulary.

Yet, there He was. Presiding.

I remember that when I'm around others: how He may be bringing me along at the exact moment I need to care for someone else…presiding.

We have no idea how even the smallest acts of concern can care for someone else for their lifetime.

I *thought* I was alone, but it wasn't true.

You may think you're alone, but it's just not true.

Grace Sandra

God presides on our worst and most important days…and more often than not, they are the same.

This was a blog post I wrote in 2015.

I used to share quite a bit on my Facebook feed, long before Instagram was The Main Thing. Long before that, was the messy-ass year of 2014, the year I left my husband of almost fifteen years. And I went ham on Facebook about it. Yes, I was that kind of Facebooker.

I was getting divorced. I chose to walk away with an agreement that we'd coparent our two beautiful boys. I'd wanted a clean cut, to run off with the man I'd fallen in love with, and to figure out how to make messy shit organized.

Cue George Oscar Bluth, "I've made a huge mistake."

Out of the clear, blue sky, my ex handed me papers asking for sole custody of our children with five, full pages of reasons why I was an unfit mother, dating back to an attempted suicide seventeen years earlier while I was in college. He'd bent details and presented his opinions as factual. I was taken off guard. I was terrified. Speechless.

When he handed me the papers, he'd asked me to do something so cliche I thought he was joking. "You should sit down," he'd said. I chuckled. I told him his nervousness was scaring me. What could possibly be so bad? I thought maybe he'd plan to stretch out the proceedings, but nothing could prepare me for those five pages.

Later, when I emailed them to one of my best friends, a clinical psychologist, she commented that that the papers made me seem like a crack whore. His influence as a minister, coupled with his financial privilege and male whiteness, meant it was very likely I could lose my boys. My babies. My sons who I loved and took care of every day of their lives. That night was the only night in my life I stayed up the entire night sobbing and wailing. The story I told myself was that I was not deserving of them, and now everyone would know why they were forcefully ripped out of my hands.

The next day, I took to Facebook and talked some shit. I vented. I lambasted his gall. But I also spoke of my pain. I wanted to articulate that it was okay for me to be heard, to be powerful, and to stand up for myself.

I wanted to acknowledge the depth of my struggles; after all, I'd left him with another man waiting in the wings—an affair that started less than two months before I moved out of our home. That man was not the reason I left, but a strong impetus to take the plunge I'd been strongly considering for years. It was too messy to come out acknowledging the affair on a Facebook status update, so I didn't. Not then. I would a few months later on my blog. As a popular-ish blogger at the time, I felt I had to explain myself. Regardless, I knew his play to get full custody was my direct punishment for the affair. But, hell, I failed at faithfulness to *him*, not my children. I understood his pain; he was being discarded. I felt empathy for him on that front, while at the same time I knew with everything in me that one does not fuck with a Mama Bear who loves and wants her cubs.

I outed myself on my blog by taking full responsibility for the affair. As much as I knew to do at the time. I barely knew how to say that our marriage as a living, breathing organism deeply wounded me. Even now, five years later, I still struggle to articulate this, if it all. I'd blogged an abiding depth of sadness, but Lord knows, I wasn't able to articulate the plethora of issues we faced.

After I shared, I felt ashamed. Bloggers call this a "vulnerability hangover," which seemed pretty all true. I shared it after tossing and turning one night. After hearing harsh words spoken about me, I wanted to rise up and defend myself.

Later, the fall out.

Immediately I lost a few Facebook friends which wasn't surprising considering I asked non-supportive friends to exit left. I acknowledged that he was a still a good man, a great father, and a fruitful minister but that he was complicated *for me.* I talked about how none of what we'd battled meant I wasn't a woman deeply in love with her children. I talked about how humans are complex. I didn't articulate any of the loving or wonderful things he'd done over the years because that's not what it was about. I didn't articulate how we fought for the good

Grace Sandra

of the other because that, too, was not what the post was about.

What it was about was this: I am here. I exist on this planet. I have a voice on this planet. I am redeemed on this planet. I deserve the air that I breathe here on the shiny blue marble. This is my perspective. I am angry. I am sad. I am frustrated. I am regretful. I have hope.

It is a.o.k for me to share my perspective on what happened to me. You were not there, *thankyouverymuch.*

This is my life, and I am not the Jezebel to his Hosea. I mentioned that little zinger in particular because that statement was made publicly. A statement made publicly—by a family member, no less—deserves to be addressed publicly. I wanted to courageously address that misstatement and the sentiment behind it.

Alongside the fall out, I received lots of rah-rah-shish-boom-bah. Plenty of "good for you, Grace!" and "Preach it, sister!" Still, the vulnerability hangover of panic, fear, and anxiety persisted into day two, day three, and day four. *Is it really worth it to open my big-ass mouth, potentially alienating our many mutual friends?* I read my angry words, and I know it was difficult to process for anyone who's close to either of us. I felt weak. When folks suggested I'd done something wrong, I'd fold like a wilted flower begging for the sun and scream out for God to revive me!

A blogging peer of mine, Nicole C., a woman I love and respect dearly, got it—not just the post, but the entire crux of my very-public writing life. She sent me a message about how brave it is to bleed out on the page as I took to doing.

She was right. I was—and am—in fact, bleeding out on the page. Bleeding. I have been writing vulnerably about my life both in blogging and in three books for years now. Have you ever asked yourself why anyone would need to keep saying publicly, "I am here. I exist. I deserve to be here?"

Hard truths are said, almost rehearsed, gritty and messy, written and cried over so that the writer can learn to believe it.

There are those of us in the world who, for whatever the reason, big and small, genuinely fight for a place to belong it. For me, it's never felt like a battle to belong in it; I've mostly been able to figure out how to exist within the normal constraints–look pretty, talk white, get an education at all costs, try to be successful, smile, shuck and jive. If you throw the extra layer of expectations from the Christian community, well, I mostly figured that out too—look pretty, but not too pretty, talk white, be appropriately charismatic, keep quiet about LGBTQ issues, and keep most sins hidden from the general public, especially *anything* having to do with sexuality. I've conformed, I've conformed, I've conformed.

The way my childhood worked against me was that upon entering adulthood, I was far too scared to exit away from the norms for fear the truth would be revealed: little Gracie Green didn't belong on this planet. Kick her the fuck out.

I've had to deal with the messages I hear and still live by. Mine are fairly sobering. It took a long time to put my finger on the "why" behind the behaviors that caused me to hurt myself—most notably, my extreme difficulty in believing this seemingly basic idea: I matter.

This, again: I am here. I exist on this planet. I have a voice on this planet. I am redeemed on this planet. I deserve the air that I breathe here on the shiny blue marble.

Grace Sandra

This is my perspective. I am angry. I am sad. I am frustrated. I am regretful. I have hope.

When I don't matter, I can't possibly defend myself without an extraordinary amount of doubt and superfluous apologies. I *want* to say I'm sorry I made someone or three feel bad while I was angrily and imperfectly trying to defend myself, but I shouldn't. I gave my one, single apology to the one about whom the post referred, and that's all the apologizing I am going to do. Anything past that is when I start apologizing for existing at all. I've been living like that for many, many years. I can't live like that anymore.

I desperately want to reach out to others who feel a deep and abiding shame in their very existence. As much as I continue to dig deep, to grasp my okay-ness in this world, I pray the act of doing so gives birth to hope. Then? Then it's worth it.

Today, while writing this post, I got this message from my friend, Chante, which brought me to tears and confirmed that I should share it:

I want to thank you for being so vulnerable and allowing peeps to see the good, bad, ugly, and fabulously great parts of your life. It's not often we get to see people really struggle with forgiveness and grace with God and others, and it is so necessary.

There's really no other good reason to write if it isn't somehow healing myself and others. It's going to be messy, y'all. It has to be.

Embrace the beautiful mess.

Messy girl
Messy hair
Messy acne

Messy faith
Messy car
Messy childhood
Messy marriage
Messy divorce
Messy explanations
Messy writing
Imperfect.
I'm here.
Showing up.
Unapologetically.
It is okay for me to exist here.
It is okay for you to love me as is.
It is okay for me to love me as is.

The following is a blog post I wrote 2 years ago.
 I know why the uncaged bird doesn't sing.
 What lurks beyond the cage I cannot say.
 I reach, but knees knock against hollowed-out bones like the hollowed heart of their carrier.
 Doors swivel, flip, revolve out of character.
 The path unclear.
 Will I fly out over, around, or under? I cannot decipher a clipped wing from a mended one.
 I am mentally trapped as a Stallion tied to a plastic patio.
 The uncaged bird doesn't sing.
 What song sings of hovering and haunting?
 Which lines describe the demonic fingers clawing against infested wounds, grasping through caged wires?

What lyrics embrace the bubbling acids of uncomfortable bellies and irregular heart palpitations catalyzed by adrenaline-laced veins?

What chorus would you add to the jittery jumps and perceived threats of violence when he gently comes in the room?

And what of the Bridge?

Shall I raise my voice in a triumphant cacophony of screeching heaves and moans?

Shall the finale please you to hear me scream and writhe for unending eternity?

Will I fly, will I fly?

No.

Not today.

I wrote his as a reflection on the haunting effects of being molested and raped by my Dad. An irritating and often misunderstood consequence is that I live in a jittery, fearful cage. If I'm in a crowded room and someone calls my name forcefully, I jump. If I'm in my house, knowing someone else is there, and they walk by unexpectedly, I jump. If I hear a noise when I'm sleeping, I shoot up. If I see a mouse out of the corner of my eye, I shriek.

What may seem like a simple threat for some, can trigger a full body reaction as if an *actual* attack is imminent. By that point, I've gone full on Jason Bourne. I'm thinking five steps ahead, my heart is pounding out of my chest, my hands are shaking, my stomach is uncomfortably turning. All of this in split seconds.

Once my second ex started his abuse in earnest, I noticed these fears kicking up significantly. I started having reactions to literally *anything*. I'd be sitting in a Starbucks, a bell would ding, and I'd startle as if a Bengal Tiger walked through the door. This was long before I received the official CPTSD diagnosis, but I knew something was horribly off. When others noticed how frightened I became at the most inconsequential activities, they'd ask with alarm, "Are you okay, Grace, o-m-g what's wrong with you?" It's only in the last year I've felt comfortable enough to tell folks. I'm living with complex post traumatic stress disorder. I startle very easily.

There are so many times my fear feels out of control. It does not feel normal to live this way.

Over the years, many have made fun of this. *It can be funny.* I get it. The shaking. The shivering. The cowering. The screaming. The jolting. Yet, I've known no other life. I have literally, for as long as I can remember, shaken, shivered, screamed, cowered, and hid. Every movie. Every television show. Every dark alley. Every parking garage. Every scary man. Other women seem to handle most of these situations just fine. It's embarrassing. I repeat the phrases, "You scared me!" or "I'm scared!" multiple times per month.

It's not something I've ever felt the agency to change, or the freedom to shake, so I do not leave my perceived cage. I do not fly most days because, surely, I will die. The alternative is to release through tears, which I have a seemingly-unending supply. Whether or not, this behavior crosses over into CPTSD, I do not know. All I know is the fear. *Some* days I struggle to push through and around it. Some days I don't. I practice various healthy, coping strategies to calm myself and work through the fears, but some days? They don't work. I press on any old ways.

I wrote this as a long Facebook status at the height of the #MeToo movement.

Years and years ago, I met with a prominent, married pastor of a large church in Detroit. I was submitting a proposal to be funded for a six-week urban plunge I was leading with the college students I was serving at the time.

When I walked in, he sat smugly behind his desk. He took me in, up and down, before commenting, "Well, look at this pretty, young thang in my office." I stood, reduced. My objectification completed in two seconds flat. The professional environment sucked from the room. My ability to articulate ripped from me. I stumbled through a well-practiced introduction as he stared at me. He did not look down.

Grace Sandra

He objectified me outright without my speaking a word, he reduced me to my looks, and set me on serious edge. From that moment on, I struggled and stumbled to be myself or even to calm myself. As I began to explain the proposal, he did not look down at the documents I'd provided for him but looked at me lustfully.

My heart was racing, and I wasn't sure what to do, so I barreled on awkwardly. After about five long, painful minutes of this, he cut me off and said, "Look, what is that you want? How much money do you want?" I asked him to consider donating to the mission trip, and he said he'd give me the amount I asked for if I promised to come back to see him, which I agreed, even though it was the last thing I wanted to do. I understood the invitation to be of an inappropriate nature. I was wearing a modest, loose-fitting, professional shirt and a loose-fitting, long skirt—not that it should matter, but for those who are still wondering if my dress somehow invited him to give me inappropriate, lustful, longing looks in a professional setting.

In another instance, I was on a date with a man when I went up to his apartment for what I assumed would be some making out. I had just arrived. I was still wearing a coat, a scarf, a hat, my gloves, and had my purse on my shoulder when we shared a brief kiss. He quickly dropped my pants and initiated sex. These are the words I said, "No," "I don't think we should do this right now," and "I don't want to do this without a condom," to which he gave three excuses and proceeded. I stood there and did not fight back. For all three minutes. Afterwards, I sat down and started to cry, and I was able to mumble out through tears, "I didn't want to do that." He said, "What? You think I raped you?" Because I didn't think of it as rape nor did I want to hurt his feelings, I said, "No, of course not." I immediately left and sat down in the elevator to cry.

What's important for me to get across in these stories is that predators know who is vulnerable and from whom they are more likely to get what they want. Like me, many women who were victims of childhood sexual abuse and molestation, violent assaults, or even severe whoopings, are much more susceptible to this type of behavior because we have zero sense of body autonomy. It's typically connected to fear of men's violation, while at the same time, desperate for men's sexual validation. It's a real mind fuck, trust me.

We have lots of stories from Gwyneth Paltrow and others who firmly and outright said "NO!" There are also those of us who have several stories of men acting badly, yet we didn't do exactly what we needed to do in order to provide enough "proof" that we didn't want it. In the second situation, I flatly told him, 'Of course you didn't rape me,' because I didn't fight back at all other than verbally. If I reported him, they'd send me home.

What we fail to realize in these scenarios is that grooming is part of the violation. I was severely sexually abused for a decade, and my abuser spent a good deal of time in the grooming process so I wouldn't fight back. One might think that's easier to do with a child than a grown woman, but that's not necessarily true when you're dealing with a woman who's been through what I've been through. I can't honestly say if I were groomed properly even now that I'd be able to handle a situation like that doing everything I'm "supposed to" be able to do.

Grace Sandra

Before you question the woman's response, actions, or push back, be careful. You may very well be gaslighting a traumatized victim.

I posted this to Facebook last year after a male friend asked me if I ever faked orgasms.

It is hilarious when men ask women if they know how to fake orgasms or if we fake orgasms. What a hoot.

As if we wouldn't know how.

Most little girls growing up knowing how to:
- fake comfortability when forced to kiss a sleezy uncle when we don't want to;
- fake a smile and laugh when someone belittles our intelligence in math or science or non-traditional "girl gifts;"
- fake blushing when someone compliments our "light skin" and "good hair" when we intuitively know we've been reduced to this tired-ass trope;

Grace Sandra

- fake silence when older men sexually violate our little bodies.
- We turn into teen girls and learn how to:
- fake being dumb so this or that boy will be less intimidated;
- fake to our teachers having to use the bathroom to escape bullying, to get a moment alone to cry it out;
- fake enjoyment when a little boy shoves his hand down there while he also fakes like he knows where a clitoris is;
- fake liking a group of mean-ass girls to try to get ahead.

Then we grow up into women who have to:
- fake like we don't hear snide comments our co-workers make about our hair;
- fake that we like women higher up the food chain, who if we piss off, will certainly get us fired;
- fake like we don't hear racist comments from men passing by on the street out of fear their vengeance might bring upon us;
- fake like we don't hear incessant cat calls;
- fake like we enjoyed pregnancy, breastfeeding, or stay-at-home mom life because mom-shaming runs deep, deep, deep;
- fake like we love a man even though we're truly we're scared of him;
- fake like we have no power because the male ego has proven toxic in our lives over and over and over and over and over again.

Do you want to know if I know how to fake an orgasm? Yeah, I know how to fake an orgasm. Most women know how to lay on our backs and fake sex all together.

Do a lot of women fake orgasms? Hell if I know. But, men, c'mon. You are truly fooling yourselves if you don't think every woman on this planet doesn't know how to fake *everything* we need to survive your gender.

In fact, most of us know how to get you to yours quicker so we can get on with our damn day. If you think anything less, you're in the sunken place.

And if you still think this post is about women faking orgasms, you're still in the sunken place.

Hashtag tired.

It was Mother's Day 2016. I was very pregnant with my third and final child, a little girl to be named Reverie. The pregnancy, and life itself, was terribly hard. I had fibroids. At least a couple, maybe three. As they grew, they pressed in on my uterus, leaving less room for my growing infant and a dull pain in my side that sometimes flared into an ongoing burning sensation. I'd had morning sickness since the seventh week of pregnancy. I threw up every day for a few reasons: either I was too hungry, too thirsty, too full, or smelled something. I'd managed to get an aversion not limited to nasty smells like baked chicken or a garbage dump, but also to smells in general.

I could throw up sitting on the toilet getting a whiff of my own shit. I'd start my business, get a whiff, and gagging would commence. Pretty soon I'd be leaning over the sink top trying to get it all out. Every bathroom trip became a bit more nerve-wracking. It got to the point that I actually tried to get through life without smelling anything.

I had sharp, shooting, sciatic nerve pain. This was the worst, as the pain left me immobilized. When my sciatica nerve started to flare, I had no fight against it. For a few weeks, I couldn't stand without excruciating pain. I'd walk around only when I absolutely had to, for food or to use the bathroom. When I'd sit down, the pain the would subside for awhile, but when I tried to get back up, it was impossible.

There were at least four occasions I got stuck in my car. Perhaps the angle of the bucket seat and how low it sat to the ground made the effort of hoisting myself and my bump up and out darn near impossible. Once, when I was stuck in the car, I called my friend Jean for no other reason than to cry. It was downpouring outside and every time I put my foot on the ground, pain shot up the back of my leg and into my back. So I put it back in. Then tried again, same thing, put it back in. This time, determined, two feet out, the upward thrust of trying to get out gave me such a sharp, shooting pain I moaned loudly, fell back into the seat, and lost my marbles.

So I sobbed. I cried about how I was stuck in the car. I cried about how bad it hurt. I cried about how hard it was raining. I cried about how when I finally made it out of the car, I'd have to slowly hobble to my front door which meant I'd be drenched, which meant I'd have to change clothes, which meant I'd have to bend over, which meant I was going to be in pain for the next foreseeable 20 to 30 minutes. I cried because I believed my new husband, whom I loved deeply, had abruptly stopped loving me.

Grace Sandra

That thought was always with me, sitting on my chest like a baby elephant.

My back had been feeling better for a few weeks. Against better judgment, I decided to participate in a mother and son dance in our church's morning services. The choreographed dance was less than three-minutes long. I'd figured out how to manage the pain by not sitting down. Every time I sat down, the pain would reset, if you will. By remaining standing until the dance, I knew I could handle it. So I did the dance with my boys in front of the church, and we survived. The moms paid $10 to wear matching, bright-red shirts with an "S" emblazoned on the front in the likeness of a Superman symbol to signify that we were SuperMoms.

I turned in the $10 late because I did not have to give. Every penny of our entire existence went to the absolute basics, and whatever we had left over went to food. It never felt like there was enough food. I was ravenously hungry every day, but also, I was specifically ravenously hungry. I didn't want a turkey sandwich. I wanted a turkey sandwich with iceberg lettuce, tomato slices, mayo, and sandwich pickles on whole wheat bread. I would often substitute getting more groceries for getting the specific groceries that would indulge both my wild pregnancy cravings and my desire for food to comfort me in every way.

The only things that truly comforted me in my pregnancy was food and sex. Both were hard to come by. I fell into the deepest bouts of self pity. Lack of these creature comforts, in particular, was the easiest, most-identifiable way to mourn all of what was happening. Oh, the downpour.

Heartache: 8 of 8

After the dance, I changed immediately into a little, tangerine maternity dress I'd found at a Goodwill for $5.99, which I felt endlessly guilty about. If you're adding that up, that's $16 on just clothing items when I routinely didn't have enough money to feed myself and my children. The dress purchase was irrational. I was confused. I felt beautiful, but at the same time, I was burdened by low self-esteem. I didn't gain an exorbitant amount of weight, and my face wasn't puffy. People told me I was a lovely pregnant woman at a regular clip. The problem was my husband almost entirely. He treated me worse than an annoying, highschool girlfriend he knocked up but could barely tolerate and couldn't kick out because he had to take responsibility for the baby. He'd spent the last six months devaluing, and eventually, discarding me—a cycle I knew nothing of at the time.

I felt a deep, pervasive sadness that he didn't find me attractive enough to touch sexually (or even non-sexually), and I thought maybe a maternity dress would help me feel better than tooling around every day in a baggy tee. When we were trying to conceive our child, I still had a well-paying job. I never thought buying maternity clothes would be an issue, but here I was, pregnant with just a few items, trying to ask as many folks as possible to give me maternity clothes or trying to find things as cheaply as possible every once in awhile. All of it sucked.

Trying to put myself together every once in a while felt mildly empowering. I even did my hair and put on makeup for selfies, which I shared religiously. After church a few of my closer friends and I were chatting. Everyone thought I looked so nice in my dress, and honestly, the compliments felt so unbelievably life-giving. The compliments, like most things in my life, were confusing as well. I tried to look nice because I desperately wanted validation for how I looked. That's something I've always enjoyed as a woman who fits squarely into traditionally-held ideas about beauty standards: light skin, long hair, pretty face. Those standards, for the record, are patently untrue. Standards of beauty can kiss my black ass and every other dark-skinned, short-haired, chubby woman who feels less than worthy for the cardinal sin of not being born white or in close enough proximity to whiteness to be considered beautiful. Nevertheless, I cannot deny that I'd routinely enjoyed the attention and privilege my looks had gotten me thus far, especially by men. To suddenly be ignored and treated badly by the man I adored in regards to my exterior was jarring as fuck.

It seemed such a chore for him to affirm or notice me that I felt like I was a burden. He would later affirm as much. At the time, he was barely pretending and not even well. His constant rejection matriculated shooting emotional pain that went well past my looks and extended into my personhood.

Who am I when my husband won't hug me, kiss me, compliment me, or initiate sex with me?

Who am I not merely as a rejected sexual being, but as a person? became a haunting question. A question that shouldn't be complicated became my obsession and a deep, festering wound by the day. I knew his distance held too much weight on my soul, but I had no idea how to distance the desperation I felt for him and the longing for some type of connection, *any* connection.

At that time, if he'd expressed excitement or even mild interest in having sex with me when I asked, that alone would have sent me soaring into the clouds. If he'd come home and sat directly next to me on the couch so our bodies were physically touching, I'd have been thrilled. I can't even imagine how happy I'd have been if he rolled over in the middle of the night to actually touch me or initiated a hug goodbye when he left for the week. I sat around thinking or googling ways I could get him to do *anything* to show me a mite of pursuit.

One day, I found a way to laugh about it. I imagined what he might do if I could stuff my horrendous, pregnant body into sexy lingerie, do a headstand against the wall, and twerk. I realized he'd probably look at me like I was ridiculous and go back to his video game. The desperation was as thorough as the humiliation. How the fuck did I get *here?* I wondered every other day.

That particular Sunday morning I felt suffocated by everything. When a few folks told me I looked great, I could feel my eyes tearing up. I was incredibly grateful to be noticed, but it was from the wrong person. At that point, my husband and I barely talked. He was away for work four nights of each week. We had a few five-minute phone conversations every day, but not much more. We'd text goodnight every night, but not much more. It seemed as if his attention was divided with someone else. Of course, I would find out later, it was. This, too, was another layer of anxiety and fear heaped onto a pile of fresh grief. So when words of life were poured into me, even superfluous musings of a distant friend, it had an affect on me.

One friend commented that my boobs looked voluptuous, that the great thing about me was that I carried the baby weight all in my belly and that I still looked sexy. I responded with the truth, *I felt sexy.*

Grace Sandra

My hormones were raging out of control whether my husband chose to indulge them or not. I felt like the embodiment of sex. I felt like the most sexual, sexualized being of all time. My sex drive was higher than it had ever been in my life. My entire life, I had never had desire quite like this. I wanted sex twice a day, at least; what I got was once a week, and I had to ask for it, even beg. Sometimes, I would try to hold out, to see if he'd come after me, but he never would. Not even a little, not at all.

I was ravenous. So, I would ask him if he would please have sex with me. He'd get this horrible, annoyed look on his face and agree, or he'd tell me he wasn't really in the mood but agree. Sometimes, he'd take a deep, huffy breath and finally agree. In a best case scenario, I'd just start kissing him to let him know it was time, and without words, he'd oblige. But his annoyance was palpable.

The humiliation of this whole process was emotionally punishing in ways I still don't know how to adequately describe. Yet, I plunged forward despite how little I felt because my body was begging me for sex, and I couldn't tell it no. Did I even know how? Is that what a sex addict would do? Anything for the fix? After it was over, my body was satiated but my mind at ill ease. He didn't always enjoy himself to climax. What kind of good-for-nothing woman can't even make her husband cum? Enter deep shame about my womanhood.

There's this horrible lie women grow up to believe: at the very least, even if all else fails, you can use your body to satisfy, manipulate, please, pleasure, or otherwise get by in life. Being sexualized from an early age in additon to my early experiences with sex in adolescence cemented this subtle message. I vividly remember my high school principal once telling me my boyfriend was addicted to my body.

I was never a woman to throw my sexuality around to get what I wanted except in one way: affection. To receive love, I would, in fact, throw my body around if it got me even a smidge of the security of love. And that strategy never failed me. Until now. There wasn't anything I could do to make this exchange, no matter how hard I tried. For the first time in my life, I changed my strategy. What if I could at least please him solely? Surely he'd see my value, my willingness to do anything, thus proving my worth as a human being and maybe even as a wife. That, too, failed miserably. There I was back at square one, but worse. I couldn't even please him to completion. As a woman, I failed. Hell, I felt my vagina had failed. From the sunken place, I felt even my pregnant body carrying a healthy child had failed.

Amidst some fear and trepidation, and even with carefully-thought-through, pre-planned words, I asked if he still found me attractive. My motivation was a deep and desperate longing for *any sort of affirmation that I was worth loving,* or even noticing. I wanted him to say one nice thing to me, just one, single nice thing. He missed the cue entirely. He criticized my questions, he confabulated my motive, he belittled my obvious vulnerability, and he reminded me he was not attracted to my pregnant body nor should he be pressured to do so.

He was cutting, sharp, defensive, and unkind. I was devastated. I hung up quickly, feigning tiredness, and cried most of that night and most of the next day. He'd chastised me harshly for my tears, and his impatience was such that I eventually hid it from him. His verbal lashing was so painful I mourned it for weeks and couldn't bring it up for months out of fear it would happen again. That was one of the first times I remember clearly wondering if he was a safe human being to be around at all. Again, I had failed. I made the monumental decision of marrying a second time and had chosen a verbal abuser who had no interest in having sex with me.

The combination of our financial struggles and my inability to secure a job—any job—made me feel like a failure. The additional feelings of failure in this realm threatened to push me right over the top.

All of this held me in a constant state of anxiety, almost panic, about my okayness in this world. I lost entire days crying, pacing, journaling, sleeping, and eating this pain. During four of the worst months of this dreadful season, I accomplished nothing but growing a child in my womb, picking my boys up from school, and trying my best to care for them during my parenting time. When my husband was home, all of my time and attention was directed at getting his attention and forcing affection while receiving contempt and horrific verbal abuse. He'd leave, and I'd spiral out into despair until he came home again. At some point, his silence, verbal abuse, and complete physical and emotional abandonment was so punishing, my suicidal ideations flared up just about every time he came home.

So there I was at church, divulging that I felt sexy while keeping my utter despair hidden. My friend responded that it was amazing that I still felt sexy, commenting that during her pregnancy she merely endured sex. I chuckled nervously, swirled with bitter jealousy. She said, "I bet he can't keep his hands off of you." What a blow. The comment stung like so many knives in my back. With gritted teeth and tears in my eyes, I said something honest, something that made the conversation awkward, something I didn't expect to say, but came out like word vomit. *Actually, I said, I'm not...* I trailed off to catch my breath before I erupted into tears and then finished...*I'm not a loved woman.*

I'm not a loved woman. A sentence that haunted me for the better part of that year.

I'm not a loved woman.

Not loved enough to be desired.

Not loved enough to be pursued.

Not loved enough to be honest with.

Not loved enough to be faithful to.

Not loved enough to speak kindly to.

I'd foolishly placed my worth entirely on his shoulders and he'd handed it back to me in ashes.

Race

A few years back, I took the Megabus Chicago to Nashville. I joked on Facebook about how all the Black-Americans on board collectively complained about how freezing cold the bus was after we had a rousing discussion of Ferguson, the protest then still in its infancy.

On the way back to Chicago, a black man in a short-sleeved tee got on the bus and yelled loudly, "It's cold as f*ck on this bus!" We all chuckled, the rest of us wearing sweatshirts, covered with blankets and head wraps and such. The man left for a few minutes and came back with an extra t-shirt. Someone joked about how he should have brought a coat. "I'm finna knit me a sweater up in this muthaf*cka is what I'm finna do!" We all died laughing, but even moreso after the woman next to him said, "And it aint finna be NO snugglin', Nigga."

Grace Sandra

Later that night, I told a friend about the jokes and the freezing cold bus. "Wait a minute." She asks, "Are those the same black folks you rode down to Nashville with?" I told her no. Remarkably, a whole new set of black folks with the exact same concerns and worries: Ferguson and the temperature of the bus, which was inexplicably climate controlled from a man sitting behind a desk three states away.

At the first stop, a white man produced a roll of duct tape. I can't make this up. A white man, mysteriously armed with Duct Tape, passed it around, helping us tape up every single vent on the back end of the bus. We joked about how our antics would suddenly produce a new warning message on the Megabus website: "New policy: no guns, knives, or duct tape on board the Megabus!" We all joked together about a made-up scenario in which the Megabus executives are sitting in a room and one says, "What did the Negroes do?" And another one says, "Um, Sir, they put up Duct Tape all over the bus, Sir. Covered every vent, Sir." We all laughed, snorting, clearly enjoying one another. All but two.

A Latino couple. They weren't laughing at all. They weren't engaging. I saw them board with their small children. Honestly, it didn't occur to me that they might not speak any English at all until I started speaking English at them. I told her—in English—how I sorry I was that I don't speak Spanish. I told her how I took it in high school and college but that I didn't remember even a smidge. I told her how we were mostly just laughing about how cold we were. I told her I wanted to be inclusive and I wished she understood the jokes. I wanted her to know I was sorry I couldn't communicate with her. She smiled. I smiled. That's all we could manage.

Race: 1 of 5

I got back to my seat and thought of my white friends—online and in person—asking me what to do about Ferguson. *"What should we do, Grace, besides retweet every doggone thing?? "I'm feeling pretty lost." "Where do I fit in in the midst of this??"*

I've given some easy answers. I've been somewhat lazy in my response to white people because what I really need to say is something entirely different.

Without even a basic grasp of the Spanish language, I couldn't explain to the Latino couple how much I wanted to include them in our lively conversation. In the case of Ferguson, not many people are going to make a real difference unless they speak the heart language of Black Americans.

White people, you won't make a difference unless deep down in your gut you have a strong sense of exasperation and anger with the fact that black men are killed at an alarming and disproportionate rate in constant discriminatory behavior.

The story of Jeremy McDole needs to break your heart. It needs to make you weep. If this man—a paraplegic in a wheelchair—had been white, he'd have been given a warning shot, a taser, a leg shot, anything else. He got a death sentence instead.

You need to feel the fear of being a mother, sister, daughter, brother, cousin, or father of a black man who you know can and will be maligned, disrespected, or killed. That fear needs to get so close to your day to day that you can't NOT think about it.

You need to absorb the emotions of being a Black American: being absolutely feared and distrusted everywhere you go. Everyday.

Grace Sandra

You need to clutch the awareness of the psychological trauma of your growing suspicions that your life has no value whatsoever. You need to allow all of that to press in on you every day for a long while. Then, you can start asking, "What do I do? What do I do??" By then, you will likely already be doing or saying *something*.

The first question I ask a white person hungry for justice is, "Have you displaced yourself?" Most of the time, the answer is no. You will never speak the heart language of Black Americans if you haven't done much to get inside the shoes of what Black Americans live every single day. If you can't displace yourself online by reading black bloggers or at the library (or Kindle shop) by reading black authors or perspectives, what makes you think you will make any sort of real difference if you can't attend an all-black church for four weeks in a row or if you actively avoid going to the black grocery store or shopping in black neighborhoods?

If you won't displace even a tiny bit, you won't learn anything about how to actually engage Black-Americans in meaningful ways. You may as well acknowledge that you're too damn afraid or lazy to allow the plight of Black-Americans to affect your day-to-day life. That is your privilege to do so. You can choose to do this and go about your business. Obviously, I hope you won't, but I've seen many white folks do just this when shit gets tough.

Black Americans are a relatively-new people group on the earth. We've only been a FREE people for less than 200 years. In terms of people groups, we are in infancy. The entirety of our tenure as a people group has been under tremendous emotional, psychological and physical suffering. We are still trying to figure ourselves out in the midst of radical changes to our human condition every fifty years for the past 300.

One thing has emerged with crystal clear clarity besides our obvious strength: the language of pain. Think of the old negro spirituals; think of the birth of jazz; think of our poetry, our rhymes, and the pain embedded in rap lyrics. If we are still evolving and stepping into our toddler-hood, still learning to walk after hundreds of years of abusive behavior, what makes you think you can formulate a to-do list and get this situation all stitched up in a jiffy?

White folks, I love y'all, but y'all are impatient when it comes to "Doing Justice." Doing Justice takes time. I know very few whites who are committed to the long-term pain and sacrifice that it takes to hitch your wagon to Black Americans when you don't have to. It will take about as much time as it would take me to relearn Spanish.

I see your overwhelm, and I get your overwhelm. When I think of the increasing numbers of sexually-trafficked young women and girls, even as an abuse survivor, I can't begin to understand what it feels like to be a homeless, eleven-year-old girl, passed around from man to man by a pimp. I am left with that same sense of hopelessness.

As a Black-American and global citizen I also feel this way about Syria, Gaza, Israel, Iraq and Iran. I know what it's like to feel oppressed, yet I don't have the first clue how to imagine living in a war-torn country. I can throw my hands up and say, *I don't understand this; I don't know what to do, so I'm going back to my everyday life. That is my privilege to do so.* At times, I have. I do. I acknowledge my privilege. I stay quiet about things I do not understand. I listen. I learn. I pray. I share. I give. I retweet. I friend. I am not the savior of Syria or all trafficked individuals.

White friends, from a basic to-do list standpoint: displace. Sit in the pain. Invest in one relationship. Give. Share. Retweet. Read. Listen. Get to know the heart language of Black Americans. I cannot imagine how different the Ferguson protests would look if even half of the Ferguson police force took this advice.

The "doing" is for those who've done the work of understanding and displacing. It's okay to not "do." It's okay for this time not to feel productive.

Sit, listen, and learn. It's truly okay.

We put on the costumes
  tryin' to fit
  suburban-hipster shit
  yo, look at me I can code switch!
  Is that *well enough* for you, Massa?
  "You don't fit here
  You don't fit nowhere but into that caricature
  Nigger, sit
  in that damn box,
  feels good to me
    IF
  I think about it."
  Groom these little boys to tone that shit down
  hair, voice, hands in pockets, smile.
  Hands on the wheel.

Grace Sandra

'Don't be back talkin' to that poooolice officer now,
ya hear?'
might wind up dead in the grave.
Trayvon will tell you
when you get there.
Learn it all.
Take it in.
Buck against.
Fall asleep
Exhausted.
Push through
  Realize
   it was true ALL along?
Yo ass is expendable.
All the n*ggers.
Expendable names
Expendable memories.
Expendable histories.
Expendable life.
Expendable death.
Put on that phuckin' costume
do yo song and dance
pretend they care
When it hits you, get comfy in that damn box,
cuz yo ass is never gettin' out.

As a little girl I knew my people were beautiful and special but also mistreated and hated. I knew I wanted to be an active part of our restoration, no matter what form that took. Dare I say, I knew at 16 years old it was my calling, though I wasn't sure how.

What my youth could not tell me was just how much *I needed to survive* to even begin having a meaningful impact. Early in my career, I was able to make a small, but noticeable difference in the lives of several Black-American college students. I spent twelve years pouring into those lives. It is still my greatest honor and life contribution to date.

Now, after wading through a divorce and a time of trauma, nothing motivates me to get my shit together more than my people and what we currently face. Noth-

Grace Sandra

ing motivates me more than the thought of joining God in what He's already doing to continue bringing hope and justice to my people.

I'm learning to view my life as a social justice advocate, a reconciler, a leader, a writer, and a challenger as a life-long marathoner, not a sprinter.

I once ran a marathon. I felt great until mile 13. I wasn't tired at all. At mile 13, though, those who were running a half marathon broke off to finish their race. I watched them cross their finish line with the cold stab of jealousy that I had to do everything I just did all over again. Even though my body felt good, my emotional state tanked.

I'm staying in this journey even though I'm tired and weak and the ghost of Sandra Bland has me weary and discouraged. It's time to buckle down for the long haul. Stabilize. Go at a comfortable pace. Stop for water. Eat. Sleep well. A life-long advocate of my people means I keep doing whatever I can, whenever I can…until I'm dead. That is my personal legacy. Not success. Not my failures (which are many). Not anything else but service. My twelve years in ministry taught me that the greatest, most effective work in being a catalyst to someone's life change is done in service with a tremendous amount of love.

Advocacy is what I love. My people are who I love. My faith is why I love. Writing and speaking (for now) is how I love. I'm teaching myself the way of peaceful protest.

Sometimes we are all in a rush to do something, not understanding the greatest clarity and energy source comes from a sharpened vision. That doesn't (often) happen overnight. I'm being pruned and torn like any leader should be. I'm praying hard that on the other side of my survival is productive work. I tire of the process, and of course, I'm angry that moral failures have cost me significant influence, energy, and time.

Thankfully, I'm in a rebirth of sorts, and the state of my people is producing a significant motivation to survive and thrive for their sake.

That's all there is for a ragamuffin like me: hope, healing, grace, and advocacy.

Unarmed, they shot you nineteen times. Gottamb.
At the hand of the three, nineteen shell casings remain on your living room floor.
They believe you were armed but found no weapon on you.

It's all a fallacy,
their belief which led to your eternal prisonment.
They believe you were armed but found no weapon on you.
Or is that, too, a lie made to cover deadly sins?
Not to worry about them: paid administrative leave.

They believe you were armed but found no weapon on you.

Race: 4 of 5

They'd been there before, seventeen times in fact.
Rage over domestic violence coursing through the veins of the familiar soldiers.
You beat her. Second-degree assault charges.
Yet, your trial ended there on your living room floor.
Three children present.
A ten year old phones 911.

They believe you were armed but found no weapon on you.

I mourn for your death,
but I mourn your life, too.
For your life and your death ended too soon.
You were 41.
You died at 8 a.m.
Your three children mourn.

I wrote this blog post in 2014.

Last Sunday, I took my boys to our new black church. When we pulled into the parking lot, Ransom (age eight and a half) sighed.

"Ugh. Mama, I don't want to go this one. I wanted to go to Daddy's (white) church!"

Rhysie (four and a half years old), of course, followed suit. "Yeah, Mama. I didn't want to go to this one."

I lug them out of the car, pontificating about having a good attitude and being thankful for all things blah blah blah when I realize I need to tell them the truth.

"Look boys, it's good for Mama to be around other black people. Mama needs more black people in her life."

"I don't like black people!" Rhysie says in a huff, stomping his foot for good measure.

I sigh. I remind myself quickly: he's four, and he does not know what in thee actual hell he's talking about. Also? I'm positive he's blissfully and conceptually challenged to what race, ethnicity, and cultural identity actually mean. After the mental check point, I kneel down to face him and smile, "Rhysie, it's not nice to say you don't like people because God made all people. All people with black skin, peach skin, yellow skin, light brown skin, reddish skin, no matter what color skin, God loves them all and we should, too."

Ransom interrupts, "Besides, Rhysie, your Mama is black. If you don't like black people, you don't like your Mama."

Rhysie looks curiously at my skin. "No, she's not; she's white like me!"

White like me.

White like me!

White like me?!

This is too much for today. Yet, attending this church is *right on time* for us three racially-ambiguous ragamuffins.

"Rhysie," I say, "Neither you or Mama are only white. God made us black, too. In fact, your Grandpa Green was black, but you never met him because he died before you were born."

"Grandpa Green *wasn't green?"*

I explain his last name was a color not a skin tone but give up when I see him fading out and spying bugs on the sidewalk.

Ransom chimes in, "Mama, I don't like this Church because... I just don't like how different..."

I tell him the first time I ever went to a big, black church, *I was scared, too.* I tell him people worship God in lots of different ways and just because we aren't used to it doesn't mean we shouldn't go to those places. I tell him I want him and Rhysie to learn to love the traditions of Black-Americans *because it's part of their heritage.*

He's either very impressed with my answer or either very bored because he takes my hand and we walk in silence.

After church, Rhysie is giddy from making Mother's Day art. Ran had an hour of snuggling, drawing, and iPad time with me during the sermon.

In the car I ask, "Now was that *soooooooooo bad?*"

Ran says no, but that he still doesn't like it.

Like most parenting moments, it's good enough for today.

I was a big ball of happy, jumbled emotions when my ex and I decided to try for our first child back in 2004. This unknown, unmade, hypothetical baby was something I'd wanted since forever. We'd been married for four years, and I begged him to start trying from the morning after the wedding. I desperately longed for a baby since I was fourteen when my raging maternal instincts kicked in. My desires for motherhood were so strong I was able to convince my high school boyfriend that we should try for a baby. And we did! At fifteen! Lord Jesus and Father in Heaven, thank you that that didn't happen.

My first husband and I married young. At twenty three, I was a new wife. Once I felt the security of a stable home and an adoring, gainfully-employed husband I was ready to procreate. My ex, however, was not. He wouldn't be ready for another four years, and it pissed me off. Between then and the birth of my first born son, I did what I could: I prayed for my unborn children religiously. I prayed for each and every one that would ever be. I hoped for three, four, or five, at least.

After the honeymoon, I drove the long way back from Detroit to haul old junk to my new home across the state. That's when I started the practice of earnestly praying for my unborn kids. I prayed for their lives, their safety, their hearts and souls, and every little thing I could think of. I decided this practice was something I should keep doing for as long as it took, not knowing how achingly long that would be: five years from that night for the first child, nine years for the second, and sixteen years for the third. Six babies and three live births. I longed for those precious, little children in those childless years. Each year that we actively avoided pregnancy, my heart grew restless.

When we finally tried, I conceived in the first month. Before I'd seen those two little lines confirming a pregnancy, a great big exhaustion had taken over. I had no idea what early-pregnancy fatigue felt like, which, for the record, is comparable to the feeling of completing a marathon, except every day for twelve weeks straight. I've run a marathon. The exhaustion levels are not dissimilar. Within a week I'd missed my visit from Aunt Flo, taken a positive test, and decided on a guiding theme for the soon-to-be nursery of Zanzibar African animals. By the next week, I'd started spotting and cramping. A few days later, I bagged a penny-sized clump to take to the doctor. The desperation of that gesture undeniably revealing. Was this clump a fetus? My baby? Here I was hoping the doctor could give me an explanation as to why I'd lost my first beloved and desired pregnancy that I earnestly prayed about for four years.

That day was December 23, 2004. I had previously planned to do all of my last minute Christmas shopping as was and is my custom. I couldn't do it. I was still physically in pain, but emotionally gutted. But Christmas. It was coming regardless of my mood. On Christmas Eve, I ventured out to the mall amidst the hustle and bustle and tried hard to push aside my emotions to get this arduous task over and done with. Each step reminding me of my current distress. I watched people smile, I noticed the flickering lights, I listened to the happiest-time-of-the-year Christmas music and I wanted to stop time to let everyone know my baby had just died. I went to the mall bathroom and heavy sobbed...*my baby just died... my baby just died. How? Why? What was the purpose?*

Even if this is an unanswerable question, the grieving, barren mother still will not hesitate to ask.

The next month, we conceived our first son who was born with great joy the next fall. A couple of years later, when I was ready for the next child, we went through the same song and dance as most couples do. In another year or so, he was ready to try, and after eight impatient months, our second son was conceived and born the next fall almost exactly four years apart from the firstborn.

When Rhys, the baby at the time, was six, he was (and is) a whirlwind of energy and emotion. Ransom, the dutiful, loving big brother, was ten. At that time, my first marriage ended. Later a new one would begin. With it, a mutual desire for one, last child. Both of us were thirty eight. Instinctively, we knew it's now or never. We began trying to conceive with gusto. It was with complete

Dem Babies: 1 of 4

shock and awe when we learned we'd conceived after one, perfectly-timed try.

After suspecting things were awry, I took a break from work to procure a quick test to confirm my suspicions. When I saw the positive test I was completely surprised and unbelievably elated. I called my new fiancé at work to deliver the news. He must have said, *"You're joking, right?"* about 5,000 times. We talked for seven minutes. We discussed approximate due dates and started planning how my maternity leave would work.

We discussed things we'd expected to deal with later, after it took forever to conceive, because that's how things work when you are considered to be geriatric. Before we hung up, he checked in to be sure I wasn't pulling a grand prank. "Baby," I said, "we've been on the phone for a full 7 minutes! What cruel woman would joke about an impending pregnancy for 7 minutes? Naw, babes, I'm forreal, forreal!"

I drove home thanking God for this beautiful gift—and after one shot! My fiance' texted me, "Just told my Mom. And my Grandma. And my best friend." He was on top of the world; this was his first biological child. We were beyond ourselves with joy.

Two weeks later, the spotting began very slowly. I was inwardly panicky, but I tried to keep my composure while I communicated to him what was happening. I thought, maybe, if I prepared his heart for the potential loss, it would hurt a little less once we knew exactly what was happening. A few days later the loss was obvious and complete. We talked. We cried. We hugged. It felt different for me this time around. Having experienced miscarriage before, the cruel familiarity of it somehow numbed the pain in a small, but noticeable way. For him, this was all new territory. This little, precious life was his first pregnancy, his first biological child, his first miscarriage.

Three weeks later, I was late. *Wait? What?!?!* A test confirmed the suspicion. I was pregnant again. I had no idea a pregnancy could happen within three weeks of a miscarriage. I took a pregnancy test in an airport bathroom upon returning from a speaking engagement. He screamed back immediately, "This is epic!" I took a seat in a quiet area of the airport, and we prayed for our little pumpkin. We prayed hard for the safety of this beloved and desired child. "I have a good feeling about this one babe," he said. "Me too!"

Within weeks I was doubled over in pain on the bathroom floor. I called my fiancé, who was early at work, listing my barrage of symptoms. "Baby, go to the E.R. Take yourself to the E.R. right now." There, I spent the next eight-to-nine hours in horrific pain, losing the baby.

The room was dark and eerily quiet. The woman performing a vaginal ultrasound was unyielding. Having her poke around in there was a gruesome experience. It felt like she was going into my uterus with a Samurai sword. I grimaced and eeked out moans of agony amidst quiet tears and emotive fears and pleading prayers: *Why is this happening again, God? Why?*

"What you are doing? It really hurts," I told her. She was cold and indifferent. "I'm sorry but I need to do it."

She poked and prodded and took her images and left my questions unanswered. I found her to be tremendously rude. She didn't want to give me hope when she could barely pick up a sign of life. But then, shockingly, she picked up what initially sounded like a tiny, little heart beat but was in actuality the sound of my own blood coursing through my body. Just briefly, hope soared. The little-zygote child was still in there but had no heartbeat. It was much too soon. In that moment, I chose to say my goodbyes.

It was a holy moment. In a moment of clarified, quiet peace, I told my baby I loved him or her and that this was goodbye. I thanked God for the joy we had while I carried that little, precious pumpkin even for the infinitesimal amount of time I was honored to do so. In the previous three weeks, I'd be been pregnant twice and lost both pregnancies.

After some time, the Big Negativity passed. The sadness smoothed out. The hope sprung up again. We began charting and testing all manner of factors, sex on schedule, hopes and prayers for another pregnancy, but this time to term. We talked about the two we lost. I checked in on him now and then because it was all so recent, new, challenging, surprising, holy, and depressing at the same time.

I took comfort in this: the ones I lost were foreknew. Prayed for. They were thoroughly loved and welcome into my body for every year that I've wanted all my babies since I was able to have babies. When we lose our babies, it's okay to ask why. Find peace in the knowledge that they were loved, seen, and wanted. What more could any living being ask for no matter how long they exist in whatever form than to be fully loved, seen, desired, and wanted?

The ones I lost are still with me. I think of them, and I love them. I always will. And those prayers? I will not stop.

Grace Sandra

*Our daughter—healthy, happy, beautiful, baby girl, Reverie—was conceived six months after the second miscarriage.

I see the curves of my breast and they please.
I see the round of my rump and it entices.
I see the button of my belly
and giggle at its cuteness.

I rub the bulging bump that
sustains my daughter;
it is tight
but lovely.

My legs are thick pillars
supporting the whole of us,
two beating hearts.

Grace Sandra

My areolas expand into flying saucers
while my nipples take on an unyielding demeanor
pushing past three sturdy layers
to embarrass me fully.
My breasts have plumped to the next cup
overflowing with milk and honey.

My face has smoothed itself
into a summery glow
while my feet have spread
into an ogre-like aura.

My hair curls tighter
while my sense of smell betrays.

I lose a few meals now and then
but this does not betray my overall impression:

I am a voluptuous, baby-making goddess.

My mind is on sex,
to desire
and be desired.

I catch my naked frame in the mirror;
it screams back to me
damn, girl, you sexy.

I glow.
I slay.
We grow.
We sway.

The whole of me is
full, filled, fantastic.
I'm a fanatical fan.

If I weren't me,
I'd want to touch me.
I'd want to caress me.
I'd want to take me in.
I'd explore every part
of this shapely missive.

But he doesn't.
He won't touch.
He won't caress.
He won't take me in.
Said my pregnant body ain't attractive.
Said I shouldn't expect it to be…to him.

At first,
I weep.
And weep.
And weep.
And weep.

Immediately,
I feel something is wrong
with me.

Ain't I nurturing a child, not a warped perspective?

I weep more.
I worry I've not taken
good enough care.

Grace Sandra

I wonder
will he find me attractive again?
will he ever see me?
will he see what lies beneath
the layers of *his child*
growing in my womb?

Is my bulging body too offensive
to have and to hold?

I don't understand.
How can this be
when *this masterpiece*
is what we both see?

Time.

No matter to me.
I won't allow the words
to burrow into my psyche
any more than the damage done.

I own this gift
whether it pleases him
is no longer of my concern
because it pleases me.

I am a LIFE-maker.
I am beautiful.
My body is a holy,
sexual temple.

Dem Babies: 2 of 4

Enter in or do not,
but leave me to love me.
I will love me
for the both of us.

3 of 4

I've wanted to breastfeed as long as I've dreamed of being a mama. In a box somewhere there is a photo of little-girl me: I'm wearing my denim overalls, flap down, smiling big as I held my favorite doll up to a flat, little-girl chest. As the last born, I never got to see Ma breastfeed my older siblings; in fact, I don't know that she did. I'm not sure where my desire to breastfeed came from. I certainly didn't see it modeled responsibly in the media, if it all. I didn't know any breastfeeding families, let alone any Black families, taking part in a larger conversation regarding breastfeeding.

My firstborn son, Ransom, was the worst nursling. Laziest latch ever. After a week, I was discouraged. *Wait, record scratch.* Let's go back to the hospital. When Ransom was just a few hours old, I was already discouraged with breastfeeding. Prior to giving birth, I had done a great deal of reading about pregnancy, labor, and childbirth, as well as breastfeeding, pumping, infant sleep training, and the challenges of returning to work in eight weeks. I was prepared, damnit! Being as prepared as I was, nothing could go wrong. Obviously. So when after a few hours I noticed a pattern between excessive cramping and putting the baby to my breast, I asked the nurse why. She explained that the breastfeeding triggers the uterus to begin shrinking, which results in period-like cramping. Somehow in my nearly-obsessive thirst for information to welcome my first child into the world, I missed that detail. Like most things that catch me off guard, I was frustrated, overly sad, and throwing pity parties of epic proportions. I wasn't emotionally ready for something I hadn't thought through. So I considered giving up breastfeeding—after about five hours.

Within eight-to-ten hours, it became very obvious that our little guy simply could not stay awake long enough to get anything down. The nurse unhelpfully recommended we supplement with formula so that his weight could be maintained at best; less drastic weight loss at worst. It was fear-based advice for an issue that would have likely resolved itself. Shoving a bottle in his mouth did nothing but cast doubt on my ability to nurture my son. Just as soon as he began drinking that first two- ounce bottle, I immediately felt that my breasts and I were no longer needed. I started wondering if I was enough for my little guy.

About a week later, we continued to have issues. He was still a sleepy, boob napper. Eating every hour on the hour before drifting off. He still had his horrible latch, and my nipples were cracked, bleeding, and lifeless. I

Grace Sandra

routinely visited the lactation consultants. I constantly read library offerings on the subject. I continued to cry my way through nursing sessions. Both the actual physical pain of nursing and the Baby Blues had taken hold of my heart, and I felt the sadness creeping always around the corner. Always waiting for me to fail.

I read a book that strongly encouraged nursing moms not to give up before forty-days postpartum. She argued that forty days was almost a magical number when many babies start to "get it," if they hadn't yet. I'd read this before he was born and had scoffed at the idea that I might give up that easily. *Pride cometh before the fall.* So even though day 20, day 25, day 30, and day 35 moderately sucked, I pushed through because I wanted to honor the wishes of the author, and I needed to believe I could pull it off for both of our sakes.

Day forty came and went with not much difference except that I had kept my goal and made a new goal to make it to eighty days. The rest is history. We kept going until he hit almost a year old when he let me know in no uncertain terms that he was completely done, *thank you very much.* His desire for his beloved sippy cup ruled the day, and just like that, my breasts were banished to normal bras and tank tops without hooks on the front.

My story with Ransom mimics many women's stories: the discouragement to give up, the need for resources, the need for lactation consultants, the necessity of breastfeeding paraphernalia like lanolin cream, breast pumps, gel soothes, nipple guards, nursing pillows, and a safe environment to nurture and nurse. I'm grateful for the awareness Black Breastfeeding Week creates to encourage Black women to breastfeed, considering many of the aforementioned breastfeeding needs go largely unmet, particularly in low income demographics.

With my second son, I made the same promise to myself to keep going until at least forty days. I sought help, and we enjoyed nearly a solid year of nursing before he, too, began pushing me away when offered. Now I sit here—at this very moment—nursing my third child, a beautiful, little girl who refuses to open her mouth very wide and enjoys a nursing session as often as I might enjoy Oreos and Almond milk, which is to say, all the time.

This third time around I suppose I feel like an old pro. There are issues of course, but she's my last, and I'm breathing in every warm moment. I'm appreciative of every coo, sigh, and suckle. I'm watching her more. I'm not wishing away this stage of exhausted delirium, and I'm making the time more meaningful. Not all the time, but most of the time. Breastfeeding is an incredible gift to us women, and there's tremendous gratitude from the bottom of my soul that I've been able to do this three times.

May my precious little diva outlast her brothers and give me a solid eighteen months. The odds are ever in her favor.

* Reverie breast fed until she was twenty-two months, and I cut her off. I wanted my boobs back.

After years and years
of angst and soul crushing sorrow,
I am at peace.
What I've been through to get here…
seems downright unmentionable.
Peace born from resolve
is greater than happiness.
But also, surprisingly there's happiness, too!

I am so in love with myself.
My boys are priceless, rowdy treasures.
And the joy of a daughter?
What three on earth could be more beautiful?
I'd give them the sun, moon, stars, and the ocean,
each and every one.

There's something different about this love I'm receiving,
this love I'm giving...
its overflowing and going out
wildly.
I'm softening to enemies,
previous abusers,
and just regular old shitty, inconsistent friends.
This love is overflowing and going out
wildly.

I'm learning to practice this: love anyway.
I'm rejecting petty,
because...God's daughter.

I'm longing for peace and reconciliation,
in new, in confusing ways.
I don't know the "how" just yet,
let me live,
let me learn.

Also? My circle. My girls.
I'd give all my toes and pinkys, too, for those babes.
When you know you would have died
without their love and support,
when you know others left
inexplicably, when you needed them the most...
The circle got smaller,
but grew in depth.

Look.
Here's what I know for sure...
Restitution is real.

Grace Sandra

Healing happens slowly.
Healing requires dangerous curiosity.
You must resolve to choose hope,
over and over again.

You must seek to conceptualize what God knows of value.
The evolution of unforced happiness isn't guaranteed.
The gift of God's mercy is beyond comprehension.
I've fought hard for this killer combination;
I couldn't be more grateful.
I couldn't be more full.

I'm alive to see another day,
after many…
…wounded.
…weary.
…wired.
…wrought.

I've been deeply hurt. Traumatized, actually.
I've deeply hurt you, him, her, them.
Deeply.
Deep breaths have been taken…
One thousand tears have been shed…
forgiveness still lingers…
there's more work to do…
(there's always more work to do).

I haven't arrived anywhere,
but I show up for the journey.
The full-on pursuit of understanding beckons daily,
the effort of healing,

the miracle of emotional and physical therapy finds me tired, but resolved.

The risk to love, to trust again has been given to God.
The words of promise have been uttered,
I do.
You do?
Because I do, too!
We do.
When it all adds up, the love overflows.
Isn't that what love is supposed to do?
No one survives trauma by themselves.
No one survives themselves by themselves.

Thank you, God.
Thank you, You.
You know if you stayed…or not.
Thank you, to those who've showed
empathy and grace
while it was still confusing.
Thank you for loving me.

No, thank you for SAVING me.
I am at peace, an embodiment of God's grace.

Actually.

THE END
~

Grace Sandra

If you enjoyed this book please leave me a review on Amazon. It helps a ton!

You can find more about my writing and future projects in my mostly sporadic newsletter. Please Subscribe Here! www.eepurl.com/dKROWg

Early next year, I'm launching a self-love + survival podcast.

My next ebook is 75% done & has a title: **Say Your Name: The Black Woman's Self-Love Survival Guide. Navigating Abuse from Black Men, our Families and Hotep Twitter in a Society Hellbent on Misogynoir.** (Release date: February 2020)

I'm also working to traditionally publish the memoir I've been tinkering away at for years detailing my life growing up in Detroit.

Lots to come. Stay updated via my newsletter! www.eepurl.com/dKROWg

Follow along on at: www.GraceActually.com
I adore social media. Find me!

My Instagram: @grace_sandra_
My Twitter: @Grace_Sandra_
My Facebook Page: @gracesandrawrites

Feel free to drop me a line: gracesandrawrites@gmail.com. I'll do my best to respond in a timely way!

Acknowledgements

Thank YOU for everyone who helped me survive the torrential storm that was 2019. There were literally so many people reaching out to me, praying for me and helping me I can't even name them all. Without all of that love, support & concern I wouldn't have survived this year, let alone pull off this project. You know who you are. I am exceedingly grateful for all of you!

To my best girls --Cindy, Jean, Marquita & Gigi y'all held it down for me! My love for y'all is infinite!

Thank you to my editor, Rebekah Gilbert who lovingly edited this compilation.

XO,
Grace

Made in the USA
Columbia, SC
13 September 2023